Michael Buzzelli

BELOW AVERAGE GENIUS

Llumina
Press

© 2012 Michael Buzzelli

All rights reserved. No part of this publication may be reproduced or transmitted in any form or by any means electronic or mechanical, including photocopy, recording, or any information storage and retrieval system, without permission in writing from the copyright owner.

ISBN: 978-1-62550-508-8 (PB)
      978-1-62550-509-5 (EB)

For my mom, Georgann, and her sisters,
Margo and Terri; my favorite audience

Foreword

Hello. I'm Mike Buzzelli. You might recognize the name from the cover. If you need to check, I'll be right here when you get back. There. That didn't take long.

Since you're kind enough to be reading the book, I thought I would officially welcome you. Welcome. Sit down. Get comfortable. It's like a party, but you don't have to get dressed up or bring a bottle of wine.

I just wanted to let you know that my opinions do sneak in here occasionally. If they offend, please skip to the next essay. I really want you to have a good time, and I don't want you stop just because you and I don't necessarily believe the same things.

Relax. Have fun. Share with friends.

Contents

Introduction	i
Come on-a My House, My House	1
Snake, Rattle and Roll	3
Lawn Trolls	5
Low Brow in High Heels	7
It's a Blurry, Blurry World	9
Hey buddy, can you spare a job?	12
I Spy Hawaii: My secret mission on the Big Island	15
Fly like a Chicken	18
A wedding and a Special Guest from a Funeral	20
Kicking the Bucket List	22
Corporate Buzzwords	24
Cookie Chaos at the Ha Ha Café	26
Champagne wishes and Caviar Dreams	30
Everything Old is New Again	32
Back to School Specials	34
All Creatures Scary and Dangerous	36
To Live and Die as a Comedian	38
Remembering the Mom and Pop Shops	40
The Whips and Chains of Comedy	42
The Customer is Never Right	44
The Pajama Game	46
Revved up Like a Deuce, Another Runner in the Night	48
The Secrets of the Universe: Revealed!	57
The Day I didn't Meet George Clooney	53
Guidance Counseling	55
The Name Game	57
Summer Loving	60
The Ripple of the Water, the Shade of the Sky are Mine	62
The Attack of the Wisp Women	64
Warning: This Story does not Contain Peanuts or Peanut By-products	66
Birthdays and Other Horror stories	68
The Fine List	70

Snapple Stories	72
Phoning it in	74
Hey Kids, Let's Make up Some Words!	76
Confessions of a Mathtard	78
Fleeing the Flea Market	80
Barbie's Dream Kitchen	83
How to say Hello to a Celebrity	85
I Got a Brand New Pair of Roller Skates	87
Terrorists Took my Fingernail Clippers	89
Artists and Their Models	91
The Further Adventures of a Name Dropper	94
Comedy, Alcoholism and sometimes Y'	96
The Bagel Experiment	98
Can't Talk Now, I Have My Foot in My Mouth	100
It's not special if it's the same old special	102
Code Talkers	105
Bad Santa	107
Past, Present and Future	109
TV Guidance	111
Nutty Health Foods	113
Misty Water-Colored Memories	115
Facing up to Facebook	117
Another Monk Moment	119
A Walk in the (Ross) Park	121
The Public Broadcasting Blues	123
The Truth About the Tooth	125
What Happened to Bubble Gum?	127
White Lies	129
Wedding Crasher	131
Casting a Spell Check	134
Below Average Genius	136

Introduction

I believe in laughter.

In our daily lives, we are bombarded by negative thoughts and negative people. Around the water cooler, we discuss war, gas prices and politics. The media is replete with grim images and tales of tragedy from around the world. We are fed a constant diet of death and destruction. Push it away. I say no more for me. There are leaner, lighter meals. I have chosen to embrace comedy.

I believe in laughter, from the giggle to the guffaw.

I believe in telling a two year-old a knock-knock joke. A small girl covers her mouth when she smiles. A young boy holds his stomach and howls. I am renewed, revitalized and ready for anything.

Laughter is not only the best medicine, it is a necessity of life, the essence of joy. The true window into our soul. When other people search their lives for meaning, I have discovered that comedy is the universal truth. It is present in even the most dour soul. Everyone wants to laugh, the saints and the sinners, the faithful and the skeptics, the Democrats and Republicans, the good, the bad, and the ugly. Especially the ugly. What else have they got?

I love a dirty limerick. A skewered song. A ribald riddle.

I believe in the Sunday comics. I kneel before the gods of stand up. I still have faith in the sitcom. I believe in the joke, the pratfall, the silly face.

Through laughter we can find the light.

COME ON-A MY HOUSE MY HOUSE

Recently, I asked a friend to a movie and she responded with, "Why go out? Why don't you just come over to my house and we can watch a movie?" I'm stuck. Now, I have to figure out a polite response without sounding like a couch potato curmudgeon.

Here's the deal. I know how to sit and watch TV. I'm very good at it, but I don't want to do anything at your house that I can do better at my house.

If I can do it in my pajamas, why should I get dressed up and come over there? If I do get dressed and go to your house now, not only am I dressed, I have lost control of the remote. I am at the mercy of your questionable taste in film and television. This is a nightmare scenario for every male I know; straight or gay, we want that remote.

If I go over to your house, I have to eat the snacks you may or may not provide. I can't go to the kitchen, find something I like and go, "Oh, little mini quiches, let's make these!"

I have to act thrilled when you put out Chex Mix.

"Oh, you made air-popped, no-salt popcorn? Awesome!" I want to add, "Can I just chew on the box it came in?" Of course, there's a chance (and it's happened before) where I go over someone's house, watch a movie, and nothing is provided but water or diet cola. No one taught social etiquette at my school, we were too busy learning algebra or geography. Our time would have been much better spent if someone sat us down and taught us that you always bring something over when you're invited to someone's house, and, if you're hosting, put something out.

I go to your house, watch what you want to watch, eat what you put out, and possibly risk getting dog and/or cat hair on my new fleece pullover.

Don't get me wrong. I love animals. I love them so much that I don't eat them (I've been a vegetarian for fifteen years). I prefer looking at them on postcards, calendars, and You Tube clips. I am not so fond of them when they are jumping up on me and humping my leg.

If I'm at your house, and the phone rings, you might, and probably will, answer it. Now, the movie, that I may or may not want to watch, is on pause while you chat with Aunt Edna. I'm stuck gazing around the living room looking for something to do, and pretending I don't hear you talking to Edna about her bursitis. The games I've come up with are; "Let's keep the cat off my lap," and "How long will the DVD stay stuck on that picture of Ryan Reynolds frozen in midair?"

I can't wait to finish the movie, drive home, plop down on my sofa, and regain control of my own precious remote.

SNAKE, RATTLE AND ROLL

"Snakes. I hate snakes." The line once uttered by a fictional archeologist/adventurer still rings true for many people. I don't hate snakes; but I have a healthy respect, i.e., fear of them.

I've had a few encounters with the slithering ophidians.

My friend Henry and I were hiking in Palm Springs. It was a hot summer day in the desert; but most of them are. We wanted to start early before it got too hot. We were the only ones on the trail this particular morning.

Suddenly, Henry began running down the path. I started yelling, "What's going on?" He was so consumed by fear, he couldn't even verbalize his predicament. He just ran and commanded me to do the same. He shouted, "Run!"

It was already ninety degrees at nine o' clock in the morning and I didn't feel like running. Then, I heard the rattle. I turned and saw an albino rattlesnake as thick as a plumbing pipe. From some reason, the glossy white skin made it scarier (if you ask me, White Snake, the band, is scary, too).

We ran a few yards away; until we could no longer hear the insidious rattle. We aborted our plans and trucked back to the car, slowly and cautiously. We practically tiptoed, as if walking between landmines.

A year prior to this incident, my aunt Terri and I were hiking in Will Rogers State Park, high above the Pacific Palisades in Southern California. It's a beautiful scenic hike along the Santa Monica Mountains, replete with cactuses and palm fronds (Will Rogers State Park is not to be confused with Will Rogers Memorial Park in Beverly Hills, where George Michael had "Fastlove" on his mind). We followed a wide horse trail all the way up, but at the top we found a divergent path cutting through the woods.

I evoked Robert Frost, "Let's take the path less traveled!" Terri nodded and we pushed back a branch and journeyed downward.

Unbeknownst to me, I walked past a diamondback. Totally beknownst (not a word, I know) to my aunt, she screamed, "Snake!"

There we stood; I was on one side of the snake and she was on the other. She wouldn't move forward to join me, and I didn't want to stroll by it again to come get her. We had a serious debate about what to do next. She wouldn't go back to the top alone, but she wouldn't move past it. We were frozen in our tracks. It made more sense for her to get bitten. I was much bigger and I could carry her; she would not be able to carry me. I was hesitant to present that as a logical argument.

Finally, I looked for a big branch, so I could fling it out of the way. Alas, there were no branches to be found. So, I grabbed a small rock. I hurtled the small rock at the snake and it disappeared into the brush. Not knowing where it was is worse than knowing where it was. This time I was the one that bellowed, "Run!"

We flew as if I were in deleted scenes from "Hidden Dragon, Crouching Tiger." Our feet only touched the earth long enough to propel us forward. I don't know if anyone saw us leaping through the woods, but I can assure you it was a dazzling sight.

We finally stopped running when we got out to the access road and encountered some fellow hikers. We felt safe enough to walk normally again. After composing ourselves, we eased on down the road. Trust me; no one would have wanted to see a large man pirouetting down the path like a fat Baryshnikov on crack.

When we got to the car, Terri commented on Will Rogers' famous quote, "He may never have met a man he didn't like, but he probably told a lot of them to 'take a hike.'"

Lawn Trolls

I am by no means a Fashionista. I don't even have my own sense of style. I'm pretty much a tee shirt and jeans guy. So, if I, with no fashion sense, see something that offends me, it must be horrendous.

On Friday at six o' clock, I saw a man cutting the grass. He had on shorts, black socks, tennis shoes and no shirt. Yes. He was shirtless. Yard work is sweaty. I don't want to think about your unprotected armpits out there in the world when you're cutting grass. It's gross.

Here's my advice, if you look like an Abercrombie and Fitch model, you may go shirtless on some occasions. If you look like Santa Claus, you should probably wear as many clothes as you can.

I would never say, "Don't be overweight." I'm saying, "Dress appropriately."

Here's the deal, everyone is allowed at the beach. I'm not discriminating against large people. I am one. I don't want to sound like a hypocrite. Dr. William Sheldon would describe me as an Endomorph. I'm fat, but I still look like a human being from far away. I only go shirtless at the beach or at a swimming pool. It is okay to be shirtless there. It's even expected. I don't like to see heavy boys in wet tee shirts at the pool. That's wrong, too. At the beach or pool, man up and be proud of your body. Besides, the wet tee shirts only make you look like you're a naughty girl on Spring Break.

As far as the black socks go, only wear them when you have a tie on. I think that's pretty clear. No matter how good looking you are; no one can pull off the shorts-with-black-socks thing. I understand you just got home from work and you want to cut the grass before nightfall, but if you have time to change your pants, you have time to change your socks. Besides, do you really want to get grass stains on your nice work socks?

That leads me to my other pet peeve about men in shorts. I hate seeing socks with sandals. It doesn't even matter what color the socks are. That's icky. No matter how attractive you are, it doesn't look good. Especially, when you have flip flops on and I can see the sock scrunched up around that rubber divider that separates the big toe from the other lesser-known toes.

I have also noticed a lot of men seem to be color blind. Yet, most of these color-blind people seem to have wives or partners. Why does the spouse not stop them from wearing some of these kaleidoscopic catastrophes? Isn't that in the marriage vows somewhere? Thou shalt not let your mate walk around in garish clown outfits. It should be. I saw a boy at a Memorial Day picnic who looked like the Skittles Rainbow puked on him. He had on green tennis shoes, bright red gabardine pants, a blue and white checkered button-down shirt and a black bandana around his forehead.

One last word of advice to my neighbor: If you want your yard to look nice, perhaps you should not be the eyesore in it.

Low Brow and High Heels

My friends and I, in our spare time, like to come up with drag queen names. Let's be clear, I have never ever worn a dress. I've never even entertained the idea. I wouldn't put on so much as a kilt, even if someone was giving out free shots of Clan MacGregor. But I love drag names.

It started innocently enough. As a child I was fascinated by puns. I remember an old Family Circus cartoon, in which cartoon character Billy, subbing for Bil Keane, drew pun-laden geography. The cartoonist named a pool of water Veronica Lake and so forth (I can't remember what was under Clark's gable).

Then years later, Harvey Fierstein introduced the world to funny drag names in "Torch Song Trilogy." Once you've heard names like Marsha Dimes and Bertha Venation, you will never be happy with a normal nom de guerre.

Years ago, I rented a beach house with some friends. I had sleep apnea so bad that I was making a low grunting noise all night long. I was heard throughout the house because of its paper thin walls. My housemates dubbed me Mona Lott. I carried the malicious moniker for years.

While chatting about the current season of Logo series' "Drag Race," my friends and I decided that the drag queens in question have uninspired names. We began to list a few of our favorites. It always starts with the most common ones like Brandy Alexander or Anita Mann and then it gets ridiculous.

The good ones range from the silly, Patty O'Furniture, to the sublime, Holly Goheavily (Capote must be looking up from hell, smiling). One erudite man in a dress picked Clare Boothe Luce Change (Trust me, Joan Crawford fans laugh hysterically). Some of them have to be spoken aloud for full impact; Rachel Tensions or Ivana Kutchakockoff.

The naming of drags is a difficult matter. You must consider what sort of performer you are going to be. For instance, if you lip-synch to Country Western ballads, perhaps Iona Trailer is the name for you. If you're on the thin side, might I suggest Anna Rexia? If you want to keep your moustache and goatee while wearing a dress, maybe you'll want to go with Tess Tosterone. Unfortunately all of these names are already taken. For the record, Miss Construe, Jean Poole, Gail Force-Winds, Helen Heels, Candy Wrapper, Kay Mart, Bea Reasonable, Layona Davenport, Winnie Baygo, Shanda Lier and Hedda Letuce are also in use. A few of them have wigged out at Wigstock.

I remember sharing the names with other friends and family. My niece even got into the act. As a child she pretended to be an entertainment reporter named Beverly Hills. The name Lois Common-Denominator made my aunt pee her pants a little.

When my friend Henry and I came across the name Helluva Bottom Carter, I laughed so hard I lost oxygen. My friend would have called paramedics for me, but he was in a similar condition. I believe I ended up on the floor of his living room in a laughing seizure. I am happy to report that we both survived the incident.

Tyler Perry made a fortune dressing up in women's clothes. I may want to reconsider my stance on never wearing a dress.

Mona Lott may have to come out of retirement.

It's a Blurry, Blurry World

I'm like Goldilocks with a camera; I've taken a lot of pictures, but none of them are quite right.

Ask my friend Henry. I took a picture of him standing next to my thumb, instead of a picture of him standing next to the guitarist of his favorite band. I also have a picture of his torso and neck at a West Hollywood Halloween parade. It's not my fault he's tall; his head didn't make it into the picture. I have to describe his costume to everyone who sees the photograph (since his head isn't in it). It was a great costume, but I guess you had to be there, since there is no recorded photograph of it.

One of the perks of my old job at the Walt Disney Company in Burbank was a free yearly pass to the parks. I took a lot of people to Disneyland when they came for a visit; but I shuddered every time I had a shutterbug on my hands. As soon as the camera came out of the carrying case, I knew I would eventually be asked to snap a quick pic. It was never quick. It was never good. Digital cameras have made the experience worse, because people can now preview the picture. In the past, months would go by before my friends/family developed the pictures and saw my photographic disasters.

Here's me at Disney; I line up the shot of my friends and/or family, I take the picture, they look at it, we take the picture again, they look at it, they line up for the shot again, repeat until exhausted. We never would get the picture perfect. Finally, no one was smiling and we called the whole thing off.

One time, I was standing in line for Magic Mountain. Somehow I had ended up alone. I don't remember the particular circumstances; but I was alone nonetheless. A romantic young couple was in line next to me. The girl was stretching her arm out as far as she could stretch to get a picture that included her head and her honey's head in the same shot. They tried to cram their heads together, until they were one weird he/she amalgam; but she couldn't get it right. Finally her boyfriend handed me the camera and said, "Do you mind?"

Frankly, I did mind. I knew it wasn't going to be any good. I have an artistic eye. I've been able to draw, paint and write poetry, but I never had the mechanical aptitude it took to work a camera. I couldn't refuse the young lovers, though.

I thought, "This time I'll take a great picture!" At least, I was always optimistic.

The couple struck a pose. I lined up the shot. I clicked. I didn't realize I hit the off button.

We laughed as we waited for the camera to warm up again. The young man pointed at the thin silver device, "Oh, see… on this camera…this is where you click." His lovely young date giggled, "I've done that, too!"

I was laughing on the outside, but I was sweating on the inside. Would my dark secret stand revealed?

On the second try, I got an extreme close up of the girl's nose. "Right. Sorry." I laughed nervously

On the third try, I hit the video button by mistake and got a short film of them holding their cutesy pose for a long time until the boy became irritated, "What the hell? It's on video mode?" They were the only words in my not-ready-for-the-Academy short.

When I hit the off button on the fourth try, the boy threw his hands up in frustration. He uttered a laundry list of swear words in my general direction.

The man in line behind us took pity on me and freed me from my Sisyphean task by offering to take the picture. "You know, I have that same camera and it is a little tricky," he said sympathetically. In one quick snap, it was done. The couple smiled at their preview screen. I was relieved.

The only thing was; I had to stand in line next to them for another forty-five minutes (the line for Magic Mountain is freaking long). Every few minutes the girl would try to catch my attention when her boyfriend wasn't looking; she was shrugging apologetically at me. I was too busy trying to avoid her gaze, fearing retribution of her partner. I anticipated riding the coaster more than ever.

I remain optimistic. Someday I will take a picture and, just like Baby Bear's porridge, chair and bed, it will be just right.

Hey Buddy Can You Spare a Job?

A lot of people I know stay at jobs they hate because they hate job hunting more than their job.

Getting a job is much more exhausting than keeping a job; blanketing the world wide web with resumes, waiting for the phone to ring, and, worst of all, putting on a tie for some yutz who doesn't appreciate it. They don't realize that it's a monumental effort to get up, get dressed and go to their office when you aren't getting paid to be there. After days of staying up late and watching Craig Ferguson, just getting out of bed early in the morning is a big deal.

I contend that looking for a job is harder than actually working at one. If I could just get a job without the prerequisite job interview, I would be fine. I hate the job interview.

When you're unemployed and looking for work, a job interview sounds exciting, until you walk in and sit down.

In California I had seen a classified ad for, what seemed to me, an exciting job; Vault Librarian for a cable channel's vast video collection. I drove down to their swanky Santa Monica headquarters and didn't even complain about buttoning that top button on my shirt so I could wear a tie.

The top button hadn't yet cut off my circulation, so I was still in a good mood when I walked up to the front desk.

I declared to the receptionist, "Hi, I'm here to see Ms. So-and-so (not her real name)."

Her mouth curled faintly, trying to fake a smile, as she guided me to a chair in the lobby. She commanded, "Sit here." I did as instructed; I can also fetch and play dead, but that wasn't in the job description.

I flipped through an ancient People magazine; Brad Pitt was still married to Jennifer Aniston, and Angelina Jolie hadn't amassed her United Nations collection of children yet.

Another potential applicant came in while I waited. The receptionist jumped out of her chair. "You must be Johnny! We heard so much about you." She was all Colgate smiles now. Johnny was wearing jeans and a t-shirt. He was late to his appointment and had to be moved back. I was early and I had a tie on. Granted, said tie was making it difficult to breathe, but I was at least dressed the part.

Johnny inquired, "Should I go in?"

The receptionist frowned, "No. Your interview is after that guy." She tossed her head in my general direction, a front header to me in an imaginary soccer game. The two of them chatted away.

Through eavesdropping, I learned that Johnny, or as I like to call him, the guy-who-wears-a-t-shirt-and-jeans-to-a-job-interview, was somehow related to someone high up in the company.

I still had to go on the job interview, even though I knew Johnny was a shoe-in.

I didn't get the job. Big surprise, right?

In most job interviews, they lob those dumb job interview questions at you. I understand the how-long-were-you-there, the why-did-you-leave and the-tell-us-about-yourself questions. I despise, "Tell us something negative about you." I want to say, "I hate being unemployed." I'm not giving up my deep darks to a total stranger, certainly not one I am trying to impress.

By the way, the interviewers can see past the old standby, "I'm a perfectionist." Real perfectionists would never admit it; they just come into the job interview and straighten the picture behind the bosses' desk, and the cat is out of the bag.

They lobbed another classic at me, "Where do you see yourself in five years?"

"Where do you see yourself in five years?" It is socially unacceptable to reply, "Anywhere but here." I want to say, "On the beach sipping margaritas bitching about your ass to the bartender?"

My brother Rick once said, "In your chair." He actually got the job. Today, he does sit in the boss's chair. I had no idea that having cantaloupe-sized cojones would work in a job interview.

If I ever go on another job interview, I'm going to have to try that sometime.

I Spy Hawaii: My Secret Mission on the Big Island

A few years ago, my friend Tom was going to a conference in Hawaii and he asked me if I wanted to come with him. Of course, I leapt at the chance to wave Aloha to LA and Aloha to Hawaii (that's goodbye and hello, respectively).

He was going on his bosses' tab. Tom was given a room with an extra bed, so it might as well be used, right? I only had to pay for my flight, meals and incidentals. It was too good of an opportunity to pass up. A week before we left, Tom's boss and wife decided to attend as well. They also realized the opportunity was too good to pass up. Unfortunately, Tom didn't want to let on that he invited a traveling companion. I wasn't to let on that I was there with him. I had to go undercover. It was a spy mission.

Tom registered and I snuck up to our room. My secret room with a view; we were in a tower overlooking the Pacific Ocean.

Tom went to the conference and I hung out at the pool. If there were wives, husbands or significant others in the pool, I wasn't supposed to say anything to any of them. I had a cover story; I just happened to be at the host hotel during their conference. I think I was allowed to use my own name. I wanted to pretend to be an English aristocrat but I couldn't keep the accent up. Even though I would pay him back, I was supposed to say I was Tom if I charged anything to the room. I didn't charge anything, but I had to say I was Tom when I got a towel for the hotel pool. Luckily, Tom did not have to explain how he was at a seminar and at the pool, simultaneously.

It worked for the most part. I would gallivant around the island, swim in the pool or ocean, and I would meet up with my best friend afterward.

Side note: If you're wondering how Tom got beat out the other competitors for the category of best friend...the answer is simple: Anyone who takes you to on vacation ranks high on the friend list, but Hawaii catapulted him into the top spot (I never screen Tom's calls, just in case he wants to take me somewhere else).

My BFF had a free day so we were going to rent a car and cruise to Pearl Harbor. Nothing says vacation like going to a war monument; a national tragedy is always good for postcards and souvenirs (too soon?).

We were standing outside of the hotel waiting for Enterprise to pick us up and take us to our rental car, when the Boss and his wife walked out of the revolving door. I had to step away from Tom. Luckily, there was a group of people milling about the front entrance of the hotel, each of them waiting for a car, cab or shuttle of some sort.

Boss and Mrs. Boss (I don't remember their names and if I did, I'd conceal it anyway) made small talk with Tom. They had rented a car from another car company, and I was standing nearby, looking nonchalant, eavesdropping.

I was standing there hoping their shuttle came before ours did. Otherwise, Tom would have to explain why some strange man was riding with him.

Then, of course, the Enterprise car showed up. I didn't know what to do. I could ride over to Enterprise, rent the car and come back for him, or just figure out a way to get him in the car. I tapped on Tom's shoulder, "Excuse me sir, but I think I heard you say that you were going to Enterprise as well?"

"Yes. Thank you." Tom repressed a giggle. I added, "We might as well ride over together." Tom nodded and bid his employer goodbye.

I got in the car and Tom followed. We didn't make eye contact or speak to one another until we were a block away. Then, we erupted in laughter. I wiped my forehead and thought of Majors Nelson and Healey after they narrowly pulled the wool over the watchful eyes of Dr. Alfred and Amanda Bellows. Most of what

I knew about Hawaii came from an episode of "I Dream of Jeannie" anyway. In it, the cast goes to the big island and Jeannie blinks a King Kamehameha statue to life.

I learned that Mr. and Mrs. Boss were also going to Pearl Harbor; so, we hiked Diamondhead instead. We went to Pearl Harbor later in the day, after we were sure they were gone.

On the last night of the conference, there was a big luau with girls doing the hula, guys fire-dancing, and lots of food and beverages. Tom thought I shouldn't miss it. We arrived separately. Tom was entertaining his employer and wife, and he was bored out of his mind. He broke off for a moment and came up to me. He wanted to be free of them. He told me that Mrs. Boss was complaining about the event; she didn't like the food, she thought that they could have done better with the entertainment, and she was particularly upset over a pack of guys from Corporate running around with water guns, shooting unsuspecting conventioneers. We were both ready to blow off the luau and party it up in downtown Waikiki; but my friend felt obligated to stay by their side as long as they attended the event, even though they were making it miserable for him.

Seconds after Tom rejoined his employer and spouse, Mrs. Boss was squirted with a mighty stream of water. The wife huffed and complained. Boss Man let out a loud expletive. They headed back to their room. Tom and I rendezvoused, grabbed a taxi, and went clubbing.

Tom never knew how she happened to get squirted right after he mentioned it to me; but it was really easy to borrow one of the water pistols. Mission accomplished.

Fly Like a Chicken

Once, I jumped out of a perfectly good airplane. I went skydiving back in the 80's. Here's how that happened: My friend Ray dared me. He was gathering a group of people up for a trip. I walked into the room when he turned to the others and said, "Mike won't go. He's too chicken."

I did my best Michael J. Fox impression and said, "Who you calling chicken?"

Of course, I had to go now. Ray had laid down the gauntlet. I should have found out what my friends were doing before I decided I wasn't a chicken. Once I found out what the plan was, I was ready to cluck a few times.

We drove up to Canton, Ohio that weekend. There were four of us...Ray, two Johns and me. We spent the day learning how to fall. I thought I knew how to fall; but the instructor opened my eyes to a whole new world of falling.

We did something called a static-line jump. Basically, your chute is attached to a cord on the plane. When you jump, the cord snaps and your chute opens. If it didn't, I was to punch the emergency chute. If the emergency chute didn't open, I was instructed to say my prayers and die with dignity.

The hardest thing we learned was folding the parachute back up and putting it in the pack. It was a lot like working at the Gap; they have their own special way of folding them. I wasn't such a good folder. Why did I think I could jump if I couldn't fold? I'll never know.

It was a windy day, and we weren't sure we were going to go up. I was getting more angry than scared. My thriftiness took over. I paid for a jump, and I was going to jump, gosh darn it (This is a G-rated book). I mean golly! It was a pricey day just to learn how to fold and fall.

Finally, the wind died down and we piled into a small plane. The plane only had a seat for the pilot; and the rest of us were scrunched in around him. I was in front next to the pilot; and I had to kneel next to the control panel. I couldn't lean forward because I would have accidentally touched something. That disaster scenario ran through my head the entire time. I tried to balance myself; touching nothing as the plane bounced around in the sky. I was so uncomfortable, I couldn't wait to get out of there.

Here's the kicker. When they called my name, I had to stand on the wing of the plane and wait for the guy to give me the "okay" signal (index finger to thumb, making a circle). That was the worst part…waiting on the wing…outside the plane. I was first. To add insult to injury, exiting a plane in mid-air is done by weight classification…from the heaviest to the lightest.

I waited out there, the wind whipping around me. I think we were 1,200 feet up (It was the early 80's, I'm surprised I remembered this much).

I jumped on cue. No hesitation. In case you guessed the ending. I lived.

The ride down to the earth wasn't that long. It was thoroughly awesome. I landed on the field not too far away from the target. I didn't end up in a tree or in the lake, and I didn't break anything.

A lot of things that are awesome are things I want to do over and over again. With skydiving, I decided that once was enough. However, if you dare me, I'd go again.

A Wedding and a Special Guest from a Funeral

Gather 'round the campfire, kids. It's time for a ghost story. This ghostly tale starts with a broken toe. I mention the toe for one reason; the skeptics can blame my spectral sighting on the hallucinatory effects of the pain in my toe. The rest of us will know the truth.

Once upon a time, my cousin Christine got married. She met and married a man named Christopher. It was the wedding of Chris and Chris. Christopher has a son from a previous relationship also named Chris. If you yell out Chris in their house, three people will answer you.

I was tasked with taking cookies over to my Aunt Theresa's (the mom of the bride) house the night before the wedding. It's a family tradition. Everyone bakes cookies for a wedding in my family; and we're gifted with the best cookie makers in Pennsylvania. Anyone who had ever eaten my Nana's chocolate chip cookies knows I'm not just boasting. I delivered a few department store shirt boxes full of chocolate chips, pizelles, and cream cakes.

I took my shoes off in my aunt's house and hit my toe against a hat rack. Two toes went one way, two toes went the other. One hit the thing dead on. I broke my middle toe. It's difficult to break a middle toe. People always assume you broke the big one, because it's the easiest target, since it's twice the size of the others. People would ask, "Which toe is it?" I didn't know. Toes don't have names. There is no ring toe, no fore toe; just the big toe and a bunch of other toes. It was the one that didn't get roast beef.

Even with a broken toe, I was determined to dance at that wedding. The next day I bandaged my toe and got to the church on time. There in the pew -- I saw the ghost of my Aunt Eleanor. Trust me, if you're going to see a ghost, the best place is at church in broad daylight surrounded by people; instead of in the middle of the night in your bed, alone.

My Aunt Eleanor was the grandmother of the bride. She was wearing a navy blue dress, a pearl necklace and reddish rimmed glasses. I remember the glasses because I thought, "You mean to tell me that when I die I still have to wear my glasses?"

I told the mother of the bride, Theresa, about my encounter with her ectoplasmic mom. It was a happy ghost story. Theresa claimed that Eleanor was buried in a navy blue dress and pearls. I didn't remember what she was wearing when she was buried; I think I was thirteen when she changed her address to Heaven.

By the way, if you're going to see a ghost, Eleanor was a good one to see. She was friendlier than Casper.

No one saw Eleanor but me. She was kind of transparent. She was standing on the side of the aisle smiling. She had a beautiful smile. Then, she disappeared. Sure, it could have been the throbbing toe, but I'm convinced she actually showed up for the wedding.

The thing is, I never saw another ghost after Eleanor. Several important people in my life have passed on since then, but I haven't seen any of them. Not that I'm actively looking for ghostly guest appearances. I don't know if there is a correlation between breaking a toe and seeing a ghost; and I'm not willing to break another toe to find out (I am picturing my friends chasing me around with a hammer saying, "I need to know where my aunt Gertrude hid her jewelry!").

Seeing a ghost is a lot like parachuting; I've done it once and survived; and I don't need to do it again.

I learned a valuable lesson from my ethereal great aunt. When I die, I want to be buried in jeans, a tee and sneakers. If I'm going to be wearing the same clothes forever, I want to be comfortable. In the meantime, I'm saving up for Lasik.

KICKING THE BUCKET LIST

Even before Jack Nicholson, Sean Hayes and that Shawshank narrator guy made the movie, I was aware of this macabre catalog called the Bucket List. Apparently everyone is dying to tell you what they want to do before they die telling you. When compiling my own list, I realized I've already had the Pu Pu platter in Life's banquet (Auntie Mame would be proud).

I've already checked a lot of stuff off my inventory. I've been to Greece, the isle of Nice and I've sipped champagne on a yacht. Thanks to yoga and meditation, I've even been to me.

I am not a list guy. Often people will ask me, "Name your top ten favorite films?" I never have an answer. If I were to compile a list, it would change almost daily.

Writing a bucket list is a curious venture for me.

I am ashamed to admit that for an Italian, I've never been to Italy. I guess that will go on my list.

I have 'learn a language' on there, too. After I got trounced in Scrabble, I realized I've forgotten a butt-load of English words. I'm thinking it's going to be harder and harder to learn another language when I'm already forgetting the only one I currently speak.

My friend Bill has "going down in a shark cage" on his To-Do-Before-Dying-Directory. I'm not afraid of too many animals; but I certainly don't want to taunt sharks from inside a steel cage. Besides when you say, "nyah, nyah, nyah, you can't get me" underwater, it's really only bubbles.

Bill's wife, Sandy, has the smallest list. She once wanted to be a tornado chaser; but a big storm put out her lights and dimmed her chances of wanting to pursue that particular dream. She also wants to see a piglet. Every time she went running off to a farm to view a piglet, the pig grew up before she could get there. I don't know why she wants to see a piglet, especially considering she once was on Atkins and ate more bacon than anyone I know. For an urban chick, she's seen "Babe" too many times.

Some people want to climb Everest. I don't want to spend my last days on the sofa, but climbing Everest sounds like way too much work. Also, I've always felt bad for the Sherpas. They do all the work and get none of the credit. The first guy to climb Everest wasn't Sir Edmund Hillary; it was some nameless Nepalese man who made the trek with Hillary while carrying a bunch of crap tied to his back. Hillary took all the credit. Blame Western Weltanschauung.

If anyone has ever heard my rendition of "Happy Birthday," they would know that singing on stage would never be on my list. Dogs commit suicide when I sing. As for playing an instrument, I once took up the saxophone. My neighbors were grateful when I put it back down.

I'm jotting down a few ideas for a revised Bucket List. The best reason for having a list of things to do before you die is to remind you to live.

Dylan Thomas once wrote, "Do not go gentle into that good night. Rage, rage against the dying light."

Now go out and live a little.

Corporate Buzzwords

I am really over corporate mumbo-jumbo. At five-thirty p.m. an accountant said to me, "At the end of the day the numbers should balance."

It was five-thirty. It was the end of the day. There was very little day left. Five-thirty was the end of my day, and the numbers didn't magically add up when I got in my car and drove home. I realize it's just something people say, but I'm not amused.

I despise corporate buzzwords. These shortcut phrases just kind of piss me off. If I ever met Stephen Covey, I'd probably have to punch him in the mouth. Don't get me wrong, it's empowering to believe you can go from the mailroom to the board of directors with a little bit of chutzpah; but the nonsense verbiage is particularly grating.

Remember when everyone was always talking about "shifting your paradigm?" I never knew what it meant. I just knew that we weren't supposed to do stuff the same old way. You know, the way that worked.

I had to think outside the box. I didn't know which box. My computer? My cubicle? There was a box somewhere and I wasn't allowed to crawl in it and think.

We used to "onboard" the new hires. All aboard! Get on the corporate cruise lines. We will be departing every morning at nine sharp and returning every evening at six or later, Monday thru Fridays, with some occasional weekend excursions.

I had to "cascade" new information to the other employees. I couldn't just tell them or send them an e-mail. Somehow, I had to cascade the information to them. Can we put this sentence in the form of a waterfall?

We had to "synergize the media platforms." Everything had to be synergized. Synergy was key. I never really got the gist of that either. Basically, everything had to work together. Of course, it is way too easy to say, "Everything has to work together."

A classic example would be at Disney, a company that owned a movie studio and an amusement park...they made a movie out of their most famous attractions. "Pirates of the Caribbean" worked; "Haunted Mansion" not so much.

The CEO is out of pocket. He is in Minnesota. We couldn't simply say, "He isn't here."

In my corporate career, I've had to "flesh out the straw man," or add details to a rough draft. Usually it was sticking an Excel chart into a PowerPoint slide and making it pretty, adding the "bells and whistles." Though, no bells and whistles were actually added, except this one time.

Someone would always say, "I don't disagree." Um. Is that the same thing as agreeing? No one wanted to actually agree because they wouldn't want to be the guy everyone blamed if the project tanked.

In every office, there's always one guy who is the magic eight ball of corporate buzzwords, repeating the corporate-speak ad infinitum as if it were his own private language. In the magic eight ball you can shake it up and see the little hexagonal die read, "Outlook is cloudy," but in the office you will hear "at the end of the day." Instead of "Try again later," you get, "Shift your paradigm." Blah, blah freaking blah. I think they're pod people cloned by the Fortune 500.

I could go on, but I have a 'hard out' at the end of this page.

COOKIE CHAOS AT THE HA HA CAFÉ

Every stand-up comedian can tell you a story about their worst night on stage. Honesty is painful and often hilarious. Why else would the Germans invent the word 'schadenfreude?'

I was scheduled to perform at "Uncle Clyde's Comedy Contest" at the Ha Ha Café in North Hollywood, hosted by Barbara Holliday and Dave Reinitz.

The owner of the club, Jack Assadorian (when he wrote down his name for me, it took me all the way to the eighth letter before I realized he wasn't writing out jackass) loaned Reinitz and Holliday the venue in the hopes of creating a crowd on a tepid weekday night.

The Clyde contest came with a hundred dollar prize, and I was eager to win. The show was a 'bringer,' and I had exhausted my list of possible attendees with numerous shows. 'Bringers' are the enemy of friends, co-workers and acquaintances who must endure sitting through your act thousands of times or resort to spouting off a myriad of excuses for why they cannot attend.

Most Angelinos just say "I'll definitely be there" with no real intention of coming (Los Angeles is the only city in America where "I flaked" is a viable excuse).

I had only one friend who I coaxed into attending on that cold and rainy night.

It was Cookie Night at "Uncle Clyde's Comedy Contest." Each night had a theme. The week before was Party Favor Night, and everyone was given a New Year's Eve noisemaker. The cacophony of noisemakers rang out during the show. It was sheer bedlam.

Still, it was nothing compared to the chaos of Cookie Night.

Below Average Genius

There were ten performers on the bill, not including the master of ceremonies. The lineup for the show was announced. I was following Jeff Pines, a comedian with a speech impediment.

Pines calls himself Speech-Impediment Man, or rather a mangled version, for obvious reasons, of the self-appointed appellation. He has made numerous appearances under the Speech-Impediment Man moniker, including the Howard Stern Show. In addition to the speech impediment, Pines is an idiot.

I'm not bitter.

Since it was Cookie Night, I bought two boxes of Archway oatmeal cookies to hand out to the audience.

A comedian, who will remain nameless (mainly because I have forgotten his name), stacked the audience with his 'bringers.' He had invited everyone he knew to the show, and they showed up. My hope of winning the hundred dollar prize money was dashed.

The contest was to be judged by the audience. I had only one friend sitting in the third row, and though he can make a lot of noise, it wasn't going to be enough. The other comedians had huge groups of support. I thought, "If everyone voted for their friend, I might get second prize." Second prize was a large plate of French fries. Yes, I am aware of the absurd disparity between first and second prize; one hundred smackers or deep-fried slivers of potato. Reinitz and Holliday couldn't be reached for comment.

The evening was a disaster. Since there was a cash prize involved, the 'bringers' were determined to laugh **only** for their friend.

Even the Emcee wasn't immune to the lack of laughter. Reinitz was sweating up on stage. The elfin jokester couldn't generate a chuckle, but the calm comedian wasn't rattled by the silence.

Pines went up and got the requisite pity laughs. Poor man has a speech impediment, but at least he's up there trying.

I'm not bitter.

Finally, it was my turn to grace the stage. It was a seven minute set and I knew I had to be fast. Upon my introduction, I started throwing the Archway oatmeal cookies into the audience. The bright lights of the stage had blinded me, and I hurled them into the void.

Wafting up from the back of the venue, I could hear audience members shouting, "Jesus!" "Ow!," and "My eye!" I was tossing the cookies a little too enthusiastically. I wounded several guests with a rain of hardened oatmeal and wrinkled raisins.

It's hard to win an audience over after you've injured them, but I tried my best. I went through a gaggle of gags to absolute silence.

Crickets and Tumbleweeds.

Nothing threw me more than silence. I began a downward spiral. This was my best material, and if I hadn't pelted the audience with oatmeal cookies, I might have been able to win some of them over.

I panicked. Odd thoughts leapt into my brain and I began verbally vomiting on stage. I uttered, "You laughed for the crippled guy," referring to Pines.

From back stage I heard, "Who you call bin cribbled? I hab a speech im-ped-dee-mint!"

It was probably the biggest laugh of the night, and, though I was on stage, I couldn't claim it as my own. I got in a shouting match with a half wit, and I was losing. I'm not bitter.

It got worse. A woman in her mid-fifties got up to use the restroom, and I blurted out, "Oh, great. Now the old lady's leaving."

She snorted back, with her hands on her hips, "Who you calling old?"

It had gotten so bad, I was berating an audience member. I profusely apologized to the woman, but it was too late. I was the masked villain in a Mexican wrestling match. But at least the silence was over.

The saddest thing is that I stayed up there the whole seven minutes (an eternity when you're dying on stage).

I had never attacked the audience before, and now I had assaulted them physically and verbally on the same night.

Needless to say, I didn't even get one French fry out of the deal. Speech Impediment Man won second prize. If there was a third prize, I didn't get that either. I'm convinced I finished at the very bottom, ten out of ten.

A young woman came up to me after the show and asked for my autograph. She was the daughter of the 'old woman.' My guess is that it was some sort of passive-aggressive onslaught on her mom. "Hey! Look ma, I have a whole Mike Buzzelli scrapbook… you know that's the guy that called you OLD in front of all those people!"

Holliday and Reinitz still host a comedy contest, but it is no longer at the Ha Ha Café. I left an indelible mark on Jack, the owner. Somewhere, above his left eyebrow.

I'm still in the game, and I can usually make the crowd laugh. What's more, I haven't injured an audience member since.

I'm knocking on wood …and I'm traveling without Archway oatmeal cookies.

Champagne Wishes and Caviar Dreams

I'll admit it. I like to go to fancy-schmancy restaurants. It's usually to celebrate some memorable occasion like Tuesday or Thursday.

My favorite place used to be Carneros Bistro in Sonoma, California. To be fair, the chef de cuisine was my cousin Janine (no, this isn't a poem). When she was making meals there, the Midnight Moon Mac and Cheese with maitake mushrooms and porcini crust was truly awesome. Also, Janine used to do something with an Heirloom tomato that is akin to magic (on the menu under "Tomato Aromatherapy"). She has since moved on to another establishment, but it was the best food I've ever eaten. I'm not sure if she makes dessert at her new restaurant, but she used to make popcorn-flavored ice cream that looks like popped kernels of popcorn, but melted in your mouth just like the creamy confection (I don't understand it, I am just reporting it).

There are a lot of great places in Sonoma and Napa, and I love a lot of them. The best thing about some of these great bistros and cuccinas is that you can basically wear anything as long as you bring your wallet.

While I love fine dining, I despise pretense. Some restaurant owners feel that they have to put on airs; some level of snobbery is involved. They enforce a dress code.

I think it's nice to get dressed up and go to a restaurant. However, I also feel that if I'm wearing a decent pair of jeans and a nice Izod, I should still get to eat indoors.

I took a friend to dinner at Madre's in Pasadena (374 miles south of Sonoma, Ca). Madre's is owned by some singer named Jennifer Lopez, who goes by the appellation, JLo, for some reason.

It was five o'clock and the restaurant had been only opened a few minutes on this particular day. The joint was deserted. The Maitre' D looked at me and went, "I'm sorry, we don't normally serve people in jeans; but we will make an exception." Let me reiterate; the restaurant was empty. They only let me and my friend in because we were the only customers. I wanted to walk out then and there; but my companion, Sandy from the 'Burgh, really wanted to dine in the singer's bistro.

Here's today's Alanis Morisette moment: The owner, JLo, has a line of clothing at K-Mart, which includes jeans. This means you can't wear JLo's clothes to JLo's restaurant. Isn't it ironic, dontcha think?

Further, the décor is shabby chic. Shabby chic is basically taking your thrift store finds and gussying them up with a fresh coat of paint or applying some trendy decoupage designs to them.

This means that my old beat up secretary desk has a better chance of getting into the restaurant than I do.

Granted, I would never wear shorts or sweatpants to a restaurant; but the jeans I had worn were a bit more expensive than anything found at K-Mart.

There are better restaurants in Northern California than in Southern California, but naturally, So Cal has to add attitude. You pay extra for attitude; it's the Hollywood way.

I recently learned that JLo's restaurant closed. I'm sticking that in my personal victory column.

Everything New is Old Again

I don't remember the day that songs from my youth ended up in elevators and on light music stations, but it happened and it's really sad. Dear Bowling for Soup, Debbie isn't the only one stuck in 1985.

I loved the 80's. I was rocking out, living large, and things were totally tubular. Yeah, we were being trickled down on by Reaganomics, but we rock and rolled all night and partied every day.

Then, the future happened. No one was looking at us in 1984, we didn't party like its 1999, and there was no space odyssey in 2001. As many older people have oft lamented before me, "It's the future and there are no jetpacks or flying cars."

My generation, and the one before it, was obsessed with stuff flying around in the sky. Blame George Jetson.

Suddenly it's today, and I'm listening to Go Go's, hanging out with friends discussing the oxymoronic appellation "Classic Pop." Can any of this stuff we listened to actually be considered classic? Our lips are sealed.

I remember the day some teenager turned to me and said, "What's an album?" I explained that in the ancient times we played music by sticking a needle on big black vinyl discs as they spun around and around, right round, on the record player, right round. It even sounded barbaric to me as I said it. Then, the teen recalled seeing these ancient record playing devices on an episode of "That 70's Show." I was mortified by his sudden revelation. The 70's are considered a long gone era. Suddenly, I am my mother explaining the expression "It's the cat's pajamas" while watching an episode of "Happy Days."

Flashback: I'm ten years old again in the back seat of my parent's car, my dad is smoking non-filtered Camels and the windows are rolled up, and we're listening to oldies. My little brother is kicking the back of my dad's fine Corinthian leather (there were no car seats). My mom is complaining about her beloved Elvis Presley being called an "oldie."

I'm Jailhouse rocked back into the present. In my head, I have a vision of the Ouroboros, the mythological serpent who swallows his own tail, and I have a revelation of my own, an asp slap, if you will; everything is cyclical.

When my mom was checking into Heartbreak Hotel, she never thought that she would be forty-something with three kids fighting in the backseat of the Chrysler Cordoba listening to the same music and being told it was old.

Someday someone, maybe the aforementioned teenager who barely remembers the word album, will be driving his own children around and the Black Eyed Peas will come on the radio and his kids will bitch and moan about being forced to listen to old people's music. "Imma be" sad, because Fergie Ferg won't be kicking it from the 21st Century into infinity.

The saddest part is it will be the future and they won't have jetpacks or flying cars either. The future will be like every other future. It will just be there like every other day, but everybody will be older.

If I live to see that day, I will still be kicking it old school, Holmes.

BACK TO SCHOOL SPECIALS

There were sighs of relief throughout the nation as kids went back to school the last couple of weeks. I know a lot of parents who were ecstatic when that first yellow school bus arrived (Fun fact: the yellow color of a school bus is called school bus yellow).

I tended to my nephew and niece, Max and Chloe, a few times throughout the summer. I had a blast hanging with them, but toward the middle of August, they were ready to go back, and I was ready for them to go back. Here's what I love about being an uncle: I love getting the kids and I love giving them back. It's a win-win!

I am concerned about those poor home-schooling parents. They will never catch a break. They don't just have them during summer and a few snow days. They have their children year round! That's terrifying!

I am fascinated by one couple in particular. They are the Duggars, and, at press time, they had nineteen children and one grandchild. The Duggars have a reality television show entitled, "Nineteen and Counting." The "Counting" because Michelle Duggar is pregnant with number twenty!

When someone tells you they have nineteen children, is there any response besides, "Yikes?"

I couldn't imagine what they go through. It is televised, but I couldn't bring myself to watch more than a few minutes of it ("Nineteen and Counting" airs on TLC and Discovery Health, check your local listings). I love kids. I really do, but more than a baseball team is too much. Apparently, the Duggars didn't listen when Dick Van Patten said, "Eight is Enough!"

I don't know many women who would let a man touch them after the sixth child. Most women I know would drug their husband's coffee; he would wake up after his vasectomy, unless they used something stronger, in which case he wouldn't wake up at all. This guy would never be heard from again. He'd just be that weird smell in the attic.

Imagine having nineteen children. Now, imagine home-schooling them. They would never leave your side. Everywhere you go, at least one of them is coming with you. It's got to be one of Dante's circles of hell. Children, like demons, circling around you for all eternity. Even if you love someone, you have to let them go away for a little while to really appreciate them.

I'm pretty concerned about the home-schooling thing. Nothing personal, but none of these reality television people seem smart enough to home school their kids.

Don't get me wrong; Michelle Duggar seems like a nice lady, but I don't think she should be teaching her kids, especially math. I'm not sure she can add, because anyone crazy enough to have nineteen to twenty kids can't truly be aware of what a large number it really is. I wonder if they have Health class. It's bad enough to hear about sex from strangers, but it would be weirder to hear about it from your parents. If they do have Health class, safe sex is definitely not in the curriculum.

I'm not against religion, but the Duggar's aren't allowed to dance. I have seen *Footloose* too many times to think that not being allowed to dance is normal. I still shake my fist at John Lithgow when he shows up in television and movies. But, hey, if you're willing to have nineteen children, you have basically created your own society and you can pretty much do what you want.

I am afraid these home-schooled kids are going to walk into a museum, see dinosaur bones and exclaim, "Ack! A dragon!"

Michelle and Jim Bob Duggar believe in Creationism. They can if they want to; but it's probably going to keep their kids out of Harvard or Yale. It might even keep them out of some community colleges.

I suppose it could be worse. If those "Jersey Shore" people have kids and home-school them, someone is just going to have to say something.

ALL CREATURES SCARY AND DANGEROUS

I love the beach. It's always a relaxing enjoyable time. Recently, I went down to Rehoboth Beach, Delaware, an artsy little beach community on the Eastern Seaboard.

That weekend, a few guys I know discovered a beached baby great white shark. They decided they would help the thing and try to get it back into the water. Yes. They were going to save the life of a shark. It was a noble idea, but, looking back, not one that I would ever attempt.

Their plan was to pick it up and swim out past the breakers and release it into the sea. It's a wonderful idea if it were a fish, dolphin or whale. I'm not convinced it was such a great idea for a shark.

I should have told them about the time I was in the pool and a bee landed in the water. It was struggling in the chlorine. I picked it out of the water to free it and it stung me. I was afraid a similar situation would occur. Only, a shark bite, even from a tiny shark, would be way worse.

Don't get me wrong. I love animals. I love animals so much that I don't eat them. I wish some of them, like sharks, afforded me the same courtesy. I've ushered spiders out of the house without killing them, but I wouldn't save a shark. I can think of a million animals I would like to save, but I don't have the capacity to love a creature that is mostly mouth.

These guys picked up the potential man-eater, which was about three feet long, and swam a few feet past the pounding surf. The shark was relatively small, but it still could have bitten off a nose, a few fingers, or any other appendage. Sure. Tycho Brahe lost part of his nose in a sword fight, so I knew that people could live without noses. You see people with missing fingers all the time. No big. It was the OTHER appendage I was worried about. I would hate to see a male friend lose the ability to pee standing up.

I can't decide if it was noble or stupid to risk your life (or, at least, valuable appendages) for a fish that could chomp on his own rescuers. Besides, once rescued, said sea creature could come back bigger next year and eat the men who saved him. I could see the headline now: Saviors become sushi.

I didn't show up to the beach until after the attempts were made to save Toothy. I've decided to give the shark a nickname (it was easier than calling him/her carcharodon carcharias).

Ironically, these would-be rescuers are not vegetarians. Matter of fact, I'm sure one of them ordered shark steak for dinner on more than one occasion. Maybe, like all fisherman, they thought they'd throw him back and wait for him to get bigger.

Toothy didn't make it. By the time my friends tried to rescue him, he didn't have the strength to swim on his own. I hate to sound like a hypocrite, but I was a little sad about it.

Rest in peace, Toothy, and thanks for not snacking on my beach buddies.

To Live and Die as a Comedian

I am somewhat of a klutz. I realize the word 'somewhat' is an understatement. It is akin to saying, "The architecture in Dubai is somewhat elaborate."

Because of the inelegant lumbering, I've had several close calls with the grim reaper. I once tripped in the street in Paris. We were steps from the Arch de Triumph, a busy intersection in the French city. I was staring at a bus barreling down in my direction. I was too startled to get up; so I rolled out of the path of the oncoming vehicle. I had narrowly escaped death, but my friends were too busy laughing to aid me.

In Greece, I misjudged my footing on the cliff at Cape Sounion and almost tumbled into the deep blue water. Luckily, a friend grabbed my arm and pulled me back. I would have died like Aegeus himself, tumbling into the briny depths. Aegeus's son, Theseus, forgot to change out the black sail on the ship, leaving his dad to believe he was dead. Aegeus couldn't bear the thought of mourning his son, so he leapt off the cliff. My death wouldn't have been as poetic; it would be from shear clumsiness.

I tripped in San Francisco walking down Market Street. Ironically, I was the sober member of our entourage: I was chastising my group of friends for getting hammered and tripped over an uneven sidewalk.

While hiking in Hawaii with my friend Tom, I tripped up the stairs on my way to the top of Diamond Head Crater. Near the top of the trail there is a rickety set of steps leading to a beautiful view of the island. In my defense, I had to answer a more pressing call of nature and rushed up to the observation deck, so I could get back down to a urinal. I would normally have stayed and admired the view, but I had to go. Tom stared down at the beauty of the island, "It's breathtaking!" I was like, "Yeah, yeah... is there a port-o-john up here?" There was not. When you're clumsy, hiking downhill under normal conditions is tricky; when you've got a full bladder and you want to run down, it's nearly impossible. I'm surprised I survived.

Yes. I've fallen all over the world. My latest close call came within a mile of my current residence.

I went for a walk the other day, and I almost bit it walking down a steep hill; ironically, I was within the view of the local hospital's emergency room entrance. I almost fell on a greasy black banana peel. Had I fallen on the peel I would have spilled into traffic and died.

It would have been a tragic yet fitting demise; the pratfall that killed. Taken out, Three Stooges style. I could envision my funeral. Everyone would be standing around sniffling until the cause of my untimely demise was revealed. "He slipped on a banana peel and died." The handkerchiefs would come out to cover the guffaws instead of the tears.

The eulogy would be "He lived and died as a comedian."

Remembering the Mom and Pop Shops

I was reminiscing with a friend about Morelli's. Back in the day, before Wal-Mart kiddies, this land was populated by mom-and-pop shops.

I loved the mom and pops. I remember going to one in Beechview, up the road from my nana's house. It's where I bought some of my first comic books and baseball cards, Adam Warlock and Manny Sanguillen, respectively. I even had a collection of Battlestar Galactica cards, back when Starbuck was a boy.

Lillian and Lou Morelli were the affable owners of Morelli's, literally the mom and a pop of the shop. I guess they didn't call them mom-and-pops for nothing. Morelli's was at the junction between Lindsay and Ursula, a stone's throw from the Scott Police Station and Municipal Building (kids, don't throw stones at the police).

I think every kid on Lindsay Road has fond memories of riding their bikes to Morelli's and grabbing some penny candy (it was never a penny, but that's what we called it for some reason).

My friend's Sheri and Gail were partial to French Onion Dip more than candy, but we all went down there for something. My mom always went for the extra-lean ground beef or the Parma sausage. Morelli's saved us from driving to the Strip on more than one occasion.

Lou was a fine, old, Italian gentleman; his wife, Lillian, was more interesting. It seemed to me that she was always dressed in a white and blue floral housecoat, like one of the Flintstone's or Jetson's she always wore the same clothes. At least, it seemed that way to me.

Lillian had an odd affectation. She used to sneak small bites of the chipped ham (Note for non-Pittsburghers: Chipped ham is deli ham sliced so ridiculously thin it comes out in shavings... sometimes called chopped ham or chipped-chopped ham).

It wasn't that she used to sneak the ham shavings, it was the way she did it. She would stare at the ceiling, unhinge her jaw like some voracious snake-like beast, and power it down her gullet, wiggling her neck as if she were some great unimaginable beast swallowing a live animal.

It was disturbing to watch, and, like a car crash, we were unable to look away. Oh you'd pretend to be looking at a can of LaSueur peas (ridiculously overpriced French peas, especially at Morelli's), but you were secretly getting some visceral thrill from watching Lil gobble the finely sliced ham bits, like the Kraken about to swallow Andromeda in "Clash of the Titans." The original, not the stupid remake.

The chipped ham never stood a chance.

While reminiscing, I realized I may not have gotten all of the details right. I'm sure Lillian Morelli had more than one outfit. Also, for the sake of full disclosure, "Clash of the Titan's" came out in 1981, after I had seen Lillian devour her prey.

Mr. Morelli passed years ago (July 6, 2001), and Morelli's General Store is now a beauty salon. Though, Mrs. Morelli is still with us.

Hide your chipped ham.

The Whips and Chains of Comedy

Comedy is a cruel mistress. One night you can tell jokes and the audience roars. Their laughter takes you away on pink fluffy clouds. The very next night you can tell the same jokes with the same inflections and intonations and the crowd stares up at you like dead presidents posing for Mt. Rushmore.

I know what they're thinking, "I just paid fourteen bucks for a gin and tonic...make me laugh, funny man." I might tickle a rib or two, and then the waitress reminds them that there is a two drink minimum.

It's really sad when you lose them. They look up expectantly, hoping for hilarity. Then, the glamour slowly wears off and they stare at you like you kicked a kitten. One wrong move, one word out of place, and they can swerve off, glancing down at their watches, trying to get the aforementioned server's attention. A furtive look and they've checked out; they just want to know when they can grab their coat and flee to the safety of the parking lot.

Even on nights when I'm on fire, I scrutinize every line, every nuance of the set. "I could have said this funnier, I could have made that gesture grander!"

It's not just me. I've watched a lot of comedian friends eat it on stage. I've seen some truly mirthful men and witty women go down in flames, Hindenburg bad.

It bothers me when fellow performers blame the audience. It's never their fault. Mostly, they came to laugh. You didn't make them smile; it's your bad, not theirs. However, I have looked out on the craggy faces of Easter Island idols and prayed that I could say something to win them over.

I had a particularly bad night and a friend will ask, "Why do you still do it?"

They remind me that public speaking is the number one fear in the country. They want to coax me out if it. Yet, they are intrigued by my ability to stand up there, fearless, in the face of possible rejection.

I like making people happy. The answer is as simple as that. Don't get me wrong, it's an ego-driven experience. When it works (and not to toot my own horn; it works with a surprisingly high success rate), there is no greater feeling than watching an audience roar with laughter (toot, toot).

There is some ephemeral link between a successful joke and a pleased audience. It is the ultimate expression of E.M. Forster's grand rule, "only connect." It is good advice, even if the title "Howard's End" produces a Beavis and Butthead giggle-fits.

I love the big laugh. The whole body quivers. It's a rush. Watching someone hold their spleen in delights me. If I can make a Malibu Bay Breeze shoot out their nostrils, I've done my job.

It's some weird sadomasochistic relationship. If a comedian does well, "he's killed," if he's done poorly, "He's dying up there." We're killing and dying. It's a violent landscape with landmines of laughter.

Come out to a show. I want to slay you in your seat. I mean that in the nicest way possible.

The Customer is Never Right

There are certain stores in America that I have vowed never to enter ever again. I don't want to name names but one store in particular bears the brunt of my ill will. I did get a good buy there, perhaps not the best buy, but their lack of customer service told me it was time to say good bye.

I never want to set foot in this particular electronics and appliance store. I hope a swanky new gadget or a cheap DVD won't lure me back into their clutches.

I have had several bad experiences there; but this one was the final straw in the coffin (whoops, I not only mixed my metaphors I threw them into a blender).

My friend Mark and I went to the store. I saw "Casablanca" on DVD in the reduced price bin. I was pretty excited about my purchase. I couldn't wait to play it again. But of all the cashiers, in all the world, I had to walk into her line. This Cashier was on the phone. She took the DVD from my hand, and scanned it. She never got off the phone. She never looked in my general direction. I wanted, at the very least, an "I'm sorry" face. You know, the I-really-have-to-take-this-but-I-want-to-help-you face. I never even got a finger. In this case, I'm referring to the index finger a person holds up to let you know that they will only be another minute. I would have loved a cup-the-phone-sorry-for-the-inconvenience speech, but that was never going to happen. No, instead, this cashier pointed at the electronic swipe-your-credit-card doohickey, without a word to me.

At first, I didn't know where she was pointing. She kept pointing, and she was getting annoyed at me for not understanding her mime routine. Luckily, I was accompanied by a friend who told me that this specific store keeps their card-reader at the end of the check-out line away from the cash register.

I swiped the card. She put the DVD in a bag and handed me a receipt, all while remaining on the phone, unapologetically. I loudly said, "Thanks for all your help," with all the sarcasm I could muster.

I didn't want her full attention, but I wanted to be noticed as a human being in the store making a purchase. The incident embarrassed my friend Mark. For some reason he decided to take her side. He interjected, "Maybe she was on the phone with her boss."

If you ever want to set off the angry Buzz bomb, take sides with rude salespeople. I bitched at Mark the whole way home. I was like, "I don't care. The boss should talk to her when she isn't on the register!"

He countered with, "Maybe it was a customer phoning in!" That made me angrier.

I retorted with, "I bothered to come all the way down to the store, why should some schmuck on the phone get preferential treatment!? I'm the one with the money in my hand. That other guy can't even get off the couch and come down for his stuff!"

Mark and I were supposed to do something after going to the store, but I told him I wasn't feeling good and I dropped him off. I didn't want him to keep excusing the cashier's rudeness, which he did all the way to the front gate of his apartment complex. I doubt he would have defended her more fiercely if she was his sister. It was nearly an ending of a beautiful friendship.

The saddest part of this story is that it was a really good price for "Casablanca."

The Pajama Game

Art Linkletter once mused, "Kids say the darnedest things!" I agree with the vaunted television host from the sixties. I've been hanging out with some friends and family these days, and their kids are cracking me up.

I took my niece and nephew to Kennywood Park, just outside of Pittsburgh, PA. Kennywood has an annual event called, "Italian Day." A slew of Italians, including many of my relatives, descended on the famous amusement park for this heralded celebration of all things Italian.

My nephew, Max, is nine and his sister, Chloe, is six. However, children under six are a few bucks cheaper at the park. So, I thought we should lie about Chloe's age. It's just a year! Don't look at me like that.

Anyway, Chloe is extremely proud of being six-years old. When we rehearsed in the car, she demanded she was six-years old. She crossed her arms and pouted, "I'm six! I'm six! I'm six!"

I insisted that she go along with my little lie. Here's something you may not know: Kids don't like to fib unless something expensive is broken.

Max proclaimed, "Chloe you're five on the way in and six on the way out."

This small chronological adjustment seemed to placate my niece and I saved a few bucks. I also couldn't stop laughing. It was a brilliant and hilarious solution. Mr. Linkletter would have loved Max.

Of course, now my money-saving plan is out in the open, Kenny the kangaroo is going to demand restitution.

Another incident happened with my cousin Elaine and her kids. I was sharing a beach rental with Elaine, her two children,

Jerry and Robert, my cousin Patricia, her husband, Todd, and their two-year old child, Dominic.

There were two bathrooms at this rental property in Virginia Beach. One was a common bathroom and the other was attached to the master bedroom. One early evening, Elaine was taking a shower in the common area bathroom and Patricia and her husband Todd were putting their son down for the night.

I turned to Elaine's kids, Jerry and Robert and said, "I sure hope your mom comes out of the shower soon, I have to use the facilities (I'm sure it was cruder than this, but I'm paraphrasing)."

Jerry said, "Just use Patricia's bathroom."

I said, "No. She and Todd are in there and they might be naked."

Jerry's eyes widened and his mouth was agape, "WHY would they be naked?"

I stumbled. I didn't want to have to be the guy that explained the birds and the bees, or God forbid, recreational sex (Editor's note: Patricia announced that she was pregnant six weeks after the trip so it was more procreation than recreation).

I covered with, "Some people don't wear pajamas."

The boys said, in unison, "Gross!"

They were fascinated by my pronouncement and couldn't believe that anyone would choose to be naked anywhere but in the shower or bathtub. I thought it was particularly funny because Patricia is strikingly beautiful and her husband is quite handsome. If they were ugly, I may have agreed with him. Instead, I was laughing my ass off.

I was already close to wetting myself, and giggling wildly did not help my situation. I sat cross-legged until Elaine emerged from the other bathroom.

I'm pretty sure Jerry and Robert's opinions about nakedness will change sometime in the next ten years. In the meantime, I'm taking my notebook to the next family get together.

"Revved Up Like a Deuce, Another Runner in the Night"

I'm not quite ready for a hearing aid, but I haven't been hearing song lyrics correctly. Apparently, I'm not the only one. Everyone has a Weird Al Yankovic buried inside them. One word of warning before you read any further: once you see the misheard version of some songs, you may never be able to sing along to the original anymore.

Back in the 80's, someone was trying to convince me that Loverboy sang, "Virgin. It's so virgin." They were really singing, "Urgent. It's so urgent." My argument was basically, "No one would use virgin in a song." Shortly thereafter Madonna came out with "Like a virgin" just to prove me wrong.

Of course, someone else misheard the words to "Like a virgin" and thought she sang, "Like a virgin touched for the thirty-first time." Of course, the lyrics are "touched for the very first time," but, for Madonna, it makes just as much sense the other way.

When I was a kid I thought Simon and Garfunkel were singing, "Can you save Rosemary in time?" It seemed logical to me. Then, I learned the actual lyrics; I couldn't believe the real words were the real words. Saving a girl from some unknown danger sounds a lot more reasonable than singing about a spice rack.

Once, a long time ago, I was adamant that Billy Joel was singing, "You make the rice, I'll make the gravy, but it just maybe be the tuna fish we're hungry for." I wasn't right, but I wasn't crazy.

Sometimes the real words are crazier. What does "revved up like a deuce" mean anyway? The Boss's "Blinded by the Light" is hugely misquoted. Modesty prevents me from telling you the most recited lyric, but it has to do with a feminine hygiene product.

Jimi Hendrix never sang "Excuse me while I kiss this guy." If he did, he would have been popular with a much different crowd.

Children screw up the words to songs all the time. For a good time, when you're with kids, turn on the radio, play a song, turn it off and ask them what the singer was singing; the results are hilarious. To a young child, "See that girl, watch her scream, kicking the dancing queen" makes much more sense when listening to Abba. At Christmas, the same child, who may or may not have anger issues, will sing, "Now bring us some friggin' pudding." It seems appropriate, especially since figgy pudding hasn't been on a menu anywhere for a hundred years. The whole point of the song is stupid, you wish me a "Merry Christmas" and now I have to bring you dessert? It doesn't sound fair.

When Eagles sing "Desperado," they do not sing, "You've been outright offensive for years now." Though, clearly, it makes more sense than riding fences. How the hell do you ride a fence anyway?

Why wouldn't someone believe that Gwen Stefani was singing, "I ain't no Harlem black girl." After all, I had to ask my niece Brittany what a Holla back girl was, but then her boyfriend called and she had to go before she could tell me.

When David Bowie went down to Suffragette City, some people thought he sang, "That yellow fat chick put a smile on my face." The real words, "This mellow-thighed chick just put my spine out of place" make much less sense.

If Tony Bennett can leave his heart in San Francisco, why can't those guys in Toto sing, "I left my brains down in Africa." Next time I hear that on the radio I am totally singing it that way.

In Elton John's "Tiny Dancer," why wouldn't we believe he says, "Hold me close, tie me down, sir?" It's more believable for Sir Elton than it is for Hendrix.

My friend Sandy is the queen of misquoted lyrics. For "Build me up, Buttercup" she thought the lyrics were "I'll be a xylophone waiting for you." I guess if you're singing to a buttercup, why not assume the songwriter can transform into a musical instrument? Actually, it's "beside the phone waiting for you," but I like to sing it Sandy's way.

She and her husband, Bill, sang a Lady Gaga song as "Bunker Face," unaware it was "Poker Face." They couldn't make out many of the words; at one point they discussed "chicken casino" as probable lyrics, which is properly translated into "like a chick in a casino." Since it is Lady Gaga it hardly counts. She sounds like she's having an epileptic seizure at the beginning of "Bad Romance."

Sandy once told me that, when she first heard it, she thought "Karma Chameleon" was "Become a comedian." More precisely, "Comma, Comma, Comma, Become a comedian." Advice I have taken to heart.

The Secrets of the Universe – Revealed!

I've had some pretty heavy conversations in my life. A lot of those late night musings with friends. In college, I used to call these 'herbally-enhanced exchanges.' My friend Brian was particularly adept at keeping me up for hours with heady thoughts rolling through my beleaguered brain.

We would have some truly twisted conversations. Topics like, "The universe is infinite, but it's expanding. What is it expanding into?"

I always liked to think of that unfinished portrait of George Washington by Gilbert Stuart, *The Athenaeum*, a picture of Washington's floating head on a blank canvas. I would love to imagine that the universe is expanding into a blank white canvas. We're some big unfinished painting by God. We would look up at the end of the known universe and ponder a conversation with God, "What's over there, God?" And God, in a deep booming voice, responds, "I haven't worked that part out yet. Get back to me in a few million years, m'kay?"

We had another thoughtful discussion over First Cause, a fairly straight-forward scientific name for the cosmological event that sparked the Big Bang. It's a classic Big Bang Theory discussion (another classic Big Bang Theory discussion was,
"Will Leonard ever sleep with Penny?" That question actually got answered in the second season).

"What caused the Big Bang in the first place?" For this answer, I liked to think of a Road Runner cartoon: Wile E. Coyote goes into a dark cave, lights a match and sees bundles upon bundles of Acme dynamite. Kaboom!

Maybe God walked into an empty universe and lit a match, just like our frequently vanquished coyote friend.

It's hard to ponder the Big Bang without God. The universe just happened to explode one day. It was just sitting there minding its own business and then...Kablewie. The only other explanation is that there was a universe before this one and someone blew it up. Maybe it was Marvin the Martian. All my answers were either God or a Warner Brothers Cartoon. Maybe Chuck Jones is God.

Brian and I spent a lot of time discussing reincarnation, too. He queried, "Do you believe in reincarnation?" Since the conversation was in a very smoky room, he asked me the same question three weeks later and I had the weirdest sense of déjà vu. Dude! Like totally.

For the record, Brian and I both believe in reincarnation. Once again, I believe, for purely theological reasons; a forgiving God would give me a 'do over.' Besides, heaven sounds boring. I can't imagine being happy forever. I think even pure bliss would get boring after the first thousand years. Does that make me a pessimist? I sort of half think so.

Some people turn to God, and some people turn to science for their answers. I was always curious why can't it be both? I choose 'all of the above.' God and science together; it's almost like one of those unlikely duos in an action comedy, like Jackie Chan and Chris Tucker.

I like 'all of the above' for the answer to everything. That way, I can marvel at the dinosaurs at the Carnegie Natural History Museum and still attend my cousin's first Holy Communion at St. Bernard's Church.

I might not know the answers, but I'm always up for some good questions.

The Day I Didn't Meet George Clooney

When I tell people I lived in Hollywood, invariably, they would ask me, "Did you ever see any famous or important people?" I had; but I always tell them about the day I didn't meet George Clooney. He's much bigger than the celebs I knew. This is my true Hollywood story.

My friend Sandy fled a dreary Pittsburgh February and came to Los Angeles. Unfortunately, we were having dreary weather in Hollywood as well. It poured down rain during most of her visit. It was unusual for Southern California, though.

Sandy came almost every year, and on every trip I became Ethel to her Lucy, as we went out hunting movie stars.

I took her out to breakfast at Hugo's in West Hollywood. Hugo's was frequented by famous people; but the menu prices were reasonable and the food was yummy. She read that Adam Sandler often trekked to Hugo's for pumpkin pancakes. I wouldn't try them, but I'm not a pancake connoisseur (the thing I always ordered there sounds equally disgusting; an omelet with spinach and goat cheese, topped with balsamic vinegar and crushed walnuts. It's actually delicious).

We entered the restaurant right at the breakfast rush. George Clooney ("Facts of Life," "E.R." and some movies) and Richard Kind ("Mad About You," "Spin City") entered right after us. Kind bitched, "It's crowded." Clooney smiled, "It's worth the wait." Clooney was kind, Kind was not. The movie star had no qualms about waiting in line like everyone else, but his friend from television was hoping to play the celebrity card.

I feel obligated to mention, both stars had tousled hair and baggy sweats on. They probably came from the gym or just rolled out of their respective beds.

I was angry with the star system at the time. I assumed that Clooney and Kind would get preferential treatment. I had been to other restaurants in the city where the stars got the star treatment. I didn't like being reminded that I wasn't even on the D-list. I was an F minus.

I took matters into my own hands and approached the podium. Kind was moving in on the Maitre' D. Meanwhile, Clooney engaged Sandy in small talk.

As I previously mentioned, it was pouring down raining in WeHo that day. Clooney turned to Sandy and said, "Terrible weather we're having." She nervously responded with, "I'm not from here. I'm from Pittsburgh."

It was more like a high pitched squeal than a verbal response. He smiled and shot back with, "I guess you're used to it then." Yes, even George Clooney knows about the weather in Pittsburgh.

At that time the Maitre D told me our table was ready. I grabbed Sandy, unaware she was yukking it up with the star of Ocean's Eleven, Twelve and Thirteen. I had a triumphant feeling; we were sitting down before the celebrities. As we walked to the table, she said, through gritted teeth, "You are taking me away from a conversation with George Clooney." She was angry up until the time her pumpkin pancakes arrived. Everyone I tell this story to responds with, "I'd be pissed at you, too!"

So, Sandy wasn't hanging with Mr. Clooney. We did have a nice breakfast. It is the most important meal of the day, you know.

Guidance Counseling

I'm having an affair with a GPS. It's like a relationship: it's constantly telling me what to do, and it always reminds me when I'm wrong. "Recalculating route" is the new "you're so stupid."

I don't even own a GPS. I rented one. I know what you're thinking, "That's so gross. You don't even know who had it before you used it."

In San Diego, I rented a GPS and got really attached. It was a Magellan. I called her Maggie. I couldn't help it she spoke to me in a British accent.

It's an amazing technological device. I plug in a location and an icy authoritarian Brit told me where to go. She even knew where the local restaurants where. For a haughty Englishwoman she really had bad taste. She kept sending me to Outback. I learned later it wasn't really her fault; San Diego is sort of a big giant strip mall. There were Outback's on every block. I just couldn't go there. I'm already one Blooming Onion away from a heart attack.

I really don't want to go anywhere without a GPS. Recently, I had a getaway weekend in Lancaster, Pennsylvania (Woo Hoo.... party all the time). It was a borrowed unit from my friend Bill. The new one also had a British woman's voice, I named her Emma. It would be wrong to give her the same name. I am always bothered when people who lose a dog go out and buy another dog and give the replacement puppy the same name. Growing up, a girl in my neighborhood had a Zeke One and Zeke Two. I just couldn't do that to my memory of Maggie. The new GPS just couldn't be Maggie II.

Emma didn't like me as much as Maggie did. Emma tried to kill me. First, she tried to tell me to turn off a bridge. She kept repeating, "Turn right now," but I was on a long-ass suspension bridge. Had I turned I would have plummeted into Susquehanna River. An hour later, she wanted me to turn on to a one-way street. The wrong way.

I tried to argue with her. The gentle English accent made me forget that Emma wasn't a real person Then, I remembered that Emma was essentially a robot, and I was arguing with a robot. I felt Luke Skywalker yelling at C3PO. Emma was completely calm. Apparently, I was the irrational one. I was having an unhealthy relationship with the technological marvel.

Since I borrowed the GPS, I locked the device up in the trunk whenever I wasn't in the car.

At a gas station I accidentally made the mistake of telling a friend to get Emma out of the trunk. I got a really weird look from the guy at the next pump. For a brief moment, I worried about having the police pulling me over and searching the car.

My advice: Be careful about naming inanimate objects: an anthropomorphic attachment could lead to counseling.

The Name Game

My brother Brian, a dolly grip for the motion picture industry, once worked on *The Mothman Prophecies* with Richard Gere. Brian had to take a day off from the film to attend the birth of his first child, Maxwell. When he came in the next day to work, *The American Gigolo* star inquired into Brian's absence.

My brother replied, "My wife had a baby. We named him Max."

Gere retorted, "My wife just had a baby, too. We named him Homer."

Brian smiled politely, but Gere must have noticed my brother's dour expression, because the *Breathless* actor added, "It's a family name."

It's not uncommon for actors to have children with uncommon names. The naming of babies is a difficult matter.

Take Apple Blythe Alison Martin, for example. She is the daughter of Academy Award winning actress Gwyneth Paltrow and rocker Chris Martin. Their child is named Apple Martin (add the letter "i" at the end and its happy hour, baby). Perhaps the *Shakespeare in Love* star pondered Juliet's speech, ""What's in a name? That which we call a rose...by any other name would smell as sweet?" If only she would have picked *any other name*.

Paltrow and Martin also have a son named Moses. At press time, Moses had yet to part his bathwater, let alone the Red Sea.

Apple and Moses aren't even the most unusual names for celebrity children. Julia Roberts has twins, Phinnaeus and Hazel, and Valerie Bertinelli has a son named Wolfgang. Hideous names, but all legitimate ones from the "Great Big Book of Baby Names." Maybe not all of them everyday sensible names, but names nonetheless.

October, 2005, Nicolas Cage named his son Kal El, after popular star of comics, movies and television, Superman. Kal El is Superman's Kryptonian birth name (the strange visitor from another planet was christened on Krypton before landing on the Smallville farm of John and Martha Kent). Wouldn't it have been easier to name him Clark? Kal El sounds Aramaic. You have to wonder how Nicolas Cage talked his wife Alice into naming their son, Kal El. Maybe it means virile in Korean.

A few years ago, Mr. Cage sold off his comic book collection. No reason was given for his decision to sell off over 400 comics, including several extremely rare and valuable ones. I suspect his wife finally figured out that their son was named after the last Kryptonian.

I imagine it's worse for the kid who has to write Kal El on the top of his homework. With luck, he sits next to Apple Martin.

Maybe Moxie Crimefighter Jillette, son of Penn Jillette, of Penn and Teller, is in Kal's class. Let that ruminate for a moment. The Las Vegas comedian/magician named his child Moxie Crimefighter. I suppose Jillette prefers his heroes to be more of the pulp variety and less of the cape wearing kind.

Actor Forest Whittaker (*The Crying Game, The Last King of Scotland*) named his son Ocean; sounds like the Whittaker family takes their names from Google maps. I surmise that when Ocean met Forest, Autumn came along (Whittaker has four children, three girls, Sonnet, True, and Autumn, and one boy, the aforementioned Ocean).

U2 Rocker Bono, AKA Paul Hewson, christened his daughter Memphis Eve Hewson. The child also has a few siblings with unique monikers, most notably Elijah Bob Patricius.

Emma Thompson (*Nanny McPhee*, and *Nanny McPhee Returns*, and about a million other movies where she doesn't have a wart on her nose) named her child after the Greek goddess of the Earth. Gaia Romilly Wise attends school in Scotland and isn't likely to have to ask to borrow a pencil from Apple, Moxie Crimefighter, or Kal El. However, she could ask her older brother, Tindyebwa

Agaba, for a ride to the nearest mall. To be fair, Emma and her husband, actor Greg Wise, adopted Tindyebwa from Rwanda and the boy already had a name.

Maybe Shakespeare wrote the stanza "What's in a name?" because he worked with a lot of actors.

SUMMER LOVING

I always think of Labor Day Weekend as a three day funeral for summer.

I admit that I am somewhat melancholy when I drive down Banksville Road and see Dormont Pool drained of the sun-dappled blue water, leaving a dry white corpse of cement.

Growing up in Pittsburgh, I learned to appreciate all the seasons, but I've always played favorites with summer.

On Memorial Day weekend, the summer is filled with hope and promise of barbecues, beaches, fireworks, baseball games, volleyball, and Italian Ice. I had a stellar summer. I went to two beaches, Rehoboth and Virginia, I got to the Scott Pool, Dormont Pool and the Settler's Cabin Wave Pool, I played volleyball (poorly) in Scheneley Park and I spent a sweltering weekend in New York City.

I think of summer as a dear friend who abandons me on Labor Day (on the last train to the coast). Now, I have to put up with her slightly annoying sibling, autumn. There will be lots of fun stuff to do in the fall. Picking out pumpkins, sleeping under the covers, and dressing up for Halloween; but I will miss summer.

The worst part about fall is that it announces the arrival of Old Man Winter all too quickly. Gotta say, "Not a fan." Is it me or doesn't it feel like winter just ended? Even after all my summer exploits, I feel like I just finished shoveling snow out of the driveway.

After living in Los Angeles for ten years, I'm excited about having the seasons back; but I'm painfully aware that winter and I haven't been on speaking terms for a decade. I have a lot of kissing up to do.

I had visited Pittsburgh for a couple of Christmases and a few weddings; but I hadn't seen snow in the last few years (except at Big Bear). It didn't take long for me to get reacquainted with winter.

I moved back to Pittsburgh in December. It was not the best time to return to the Steel City. I remember I missed the first snowfall and I was a little disappointed. I didn't miss it for long. Shortly after I arrived, it snowed again. And again. And again. It continued to snow day after day from December '09 until March '10. I was over it.

I happily shoveled the driveway on my first snowfall. I was glad to be outside working up a sweat. I was enjoying the flakes as they fell. The next day, I was a little less enthused. The day after that, I was starting to develop an attitude. By mid-February, I hoped never to see the flaky white powder ever again, but it kept coming. Toward the end of February, I thought I would never see sunshine again. For the shortest month, February sure seemed like the longest. July and August may have 31 days, but they zoomed by, compared to the glacial (pun always intended) speed of February.

I am optimistic about having a pleasant autumn. I'll be leaf-peeping with the best of them; but in the back of my mind I will be thinking about the coming onslaught of cold and snow.

I intend to embrace winter. I'm going to fill it up with a few ski trips, some sled riding/tubing and a few snowball fights.

I am trying to make friends with winter; but I expect I'll get the cold shoulder.

"The ripple of the Water, the Shade of the Sky are Mine"

Once upon a time, my aunt Terri and I went to this hoity-toity restaurant in Malibu. We dined el fresco, and the view from the table was spectacular, gazing on the Pacific Ocean. The view was by far the best part of our evening. Our server was so annoying he ruined my enjoyment of the dinner. Clearly, he was a failed actor making the most of his role of a lifetime: Pretentious Waiter.

I ordered the shrimp primavera without the shrimp. However, we ended up paying for the shrimp I didn't get. Note to restaurant goers: They don't adjust the price when they take out an ingredient; they just jack up a price if they add something. It wasn't fair; but I didn't realize that until we had gotten the bill. Had I known, I would have ordered the shrimp on the side and given them away. Some homeless man would have had the catch of the day (Terri didn't eat seafood either or I would have handed the little pink prawns over to her).

The waiter also talked me into getting bottled water for the table. Here's the deal, I always drink bottled water. This, however, was water bottled in Italy and it came with an import price (it wasn't cheap). I don't think we should have to pay more than a few dollars for water. When did we start paying extra for essentials like water? It was flat water, no bubbles. I would have paid extra for bubbles. I like Perrier and I don't mind paying for the carbonation, which is essentially extra air. I like the extra air, though.

In Europe when you ask for water they say, "Gas or no gas?" Meaning with bubbles or without. I seem to think the bartenders are commenting on the state of your gastrointestinal system after consuming said product.

Once, I went to the Oxygen Bar on Sunset where I paid good money for air. They must have seen me coming. I was puffing on a breath of pure oxygen, and a man and his young son walked by the front window. I imagined a conversation between them:

The boy would query, "What do they sell in there, daddy?"

The father would scratch his chin and reply, "Air, son."

The boy would tilt his head like a puppy, trying to grasp his father's answer, "Don't we get that for free?"

The father, realizing he is trapped in one of those why-is-the-sky-blue moments, would stare at the boy and say, "Don't ask so many questions!"

The father would then pull his boy down the street. Maybe they'd end up on Hollywood Boulevard where the dad could explain prostitution to his child. Prostitution would, at least, make more sense.

I've heard they pump oxygen into the casinos in Las Vegas so you feel more awake. I always feel energized in Vegas so I'm willing to believe it is true. The only other logical explanation for my increased energy level at the Bellagio would be that I have a gambling problem. Though, I am willing to bet money that I don't.

Somewhere Native Americans are laughing at us, because we pay for water and air. Of course, now we're gambling in their casinos.

The Attack of the Wisp Women

Girl Math: If five heterosexual women go away for a ski weekend to a cabin with six bedrooms, how many bedrooms are used? If you guessed three, place a gold star on your forehead.

The real answer was an even more complicated math problem. On the first night, three bedrooms were used. On the next night, two bedrooms were used. On the last night the whole gang all piled together on a California King.

The aforementioned women decided it would be cuter and more fun if they shared the bedrooms instead of each sleeping in their own beds. It was a giant slumber party replete with chile con queso and Pina Coladas.

I accompanied the eponymous five women on their trip to the Wisp Ski Resort on the edge of Maryland. My friend Heidi owns and operates two stores and a kiosk in Orlando, Florida (www.polkadotz.com). When the stores hit a milestone sales goal, she took four of her employees (three managers and an assistant manager) away for a weekend. Heidi's girls were Latina and many of them had never skied. Actually, many of them had never even seen snow. A few days before the ski weekend, Heidi called me up and asked me to join them and I did. Hilarity ensued.

There were no pillow fights or practice French kissing sessions, but there was a lot of giggling. I did hang out on the edge of a few beds laughing and carrying on, but I always retreated to my separate sleeping quarters on another floor of the cabin. We were joined by a few other visitors, but since the girls were sharing there was plenty of space for more guests.

Adult sleepovers are the line of demarcation between the sexes. No man gets into a bed with anyone unless he's up to something naughty. A straight guy isn't going to have any male friends sleep over. The only exception to this rule is when a buddy is so slobber-knockered he passes out on your couch. There would be no bed sharing, unless the aforementioned straight guy isn't completely straight about being straight.

I have noticed that women go to nightclubs and dance with each other. Heterosexual men do not ask their friends out on the dance floor. For some reason, weddings seem to be exempt from this rule (maybe because bride and groom have already paid the bar tab).

In my travels, I have also noticed that girls will make out with each other to get the attention of a man. It doesn't work out in reverse. You will never see a guy turn to a friend and say, "Hey Tom, that chick is looking over here. Quick, let's make out!" It has happened at a few bars I've been to, but the kissing couple really wasn't seeking the attention of the girl who was watching them.

There are a lot of theories on the difference between the sexes. Overall I think a woman can do anything a man can do, except pee standing up. There are, however, a few things women can do that men can't, and one of them is having an adult slumber party. Guys, you don't know what you're missing.

Warning: This Story Does Not Contain Peanuts or Peanut By-Products

A few weeks ago, I had a terrible cold and I couldn't sleep. I reached out for a product that I hoped would alleviate my sniffling, sneezing, coughing, and aching symptoms. I reached for the Nyquil; so I could sleep.

I turned bottle over and read, "Warning: May cause drowsiness." It's Nyquil. That was the point. I rolled my eyes and sighed. It's just another there-are-instructions-on-the-shampoo-bottle moment.

We live in a society that warns us that our hot coffee may be hot.

Everyone blames the lawyers. I don't. I blame the dumb bunnies who sipped the coffee and burned themselves in the first place. I blame the guy who must have taken Nyquil before going to work and/or operating heavy machinery; he could have gone with Dayquil (That's why the lovely people at Vicks make both Day and Night versions). I blame the person who looked at the bottle of shampoo and said, "I have no idea what to do with this."

Companies have to slap all these warnings on products or something will go horribly wrong. I know this to be true. I read the Darwin Awards. Every year, someone inevitably does something so stupid that they die from not reading the label. Recently, I heard about the criminal who spray-painted himself gold. The gold paint was used as a disguise so that he and his friend could rob the Sprint store. He fled with cash and credit cards, but died of asphyxiation because he didn't read the warning on the metallic paint; it was highly toxic.

If we didn't have labels, there would be so many more tragic deaths. We would be mourning the loss of people who plummet to their death in Superman costumes because they didn't read the label that clearly stated, "Wearing of this garment does not enable you to fly."

A portable stroller advises, "Caution: Remove infant before folding for storage." I sure hope busy moms take the time to read that label, or they'll have trouble distinguishing their baby from their accordion.

A can of pepper spray is labeled, "May irritate eyes." I should hope so. If I pepper spray a would-be assailant, I don't want my attacker to say, "My goodness, sir! That was mildly unpleasant," or whatever it is they're saying on the street these days.

"Do not use orally," is good advice, especially when said advice is on the handle of a toilet brush.

I do worry about the unfortunate woman that does not heed the warning on her curling iron, "For external use only!" There is going to be a hot time in the old town tonight.

This groundbreaking tidbit appears on an inordinate amount of products, "Do not use while sleeping or unconscious." I find it so hard to use products when I'm sleeping or unconscious.

Some labels do confuse me, though. My string of Christmas lights warns, "For indoor or outdoor use only." If I'm not indoors or outdoors where the heck am I? If I ever end up in this neither region between indoors and outdoors, I better not bring the Christmas lights with me.

BIRTHDAYS AND OTHER HORROR STORIES

Birthdays are such a happy occasion…when you're twelve. They seem to get worse and worse, especially after turning twenty-one. I turned twenty-one in the ancient times, kids, in the late Mesozoic. My worst birthday was my thirty-ninth one. After I blew out the candles, I spent the next 365 days worrying about turning forty. It was a milestone I wasn't willing to face. There were myriad reasons why I dreaded the big four-oh. I think it was that shiny helium balloon that said, "Lordy, Lordy, look who's forty!"

Mostly, it was because I was, and still am, single. Though ask me my real age now and I will say, "You have to cut me open and count the rings." When I was thirty-nine I was searching potential mates on the Internet, and all of the Match.com ads read, "Looking for someone between the ages of 25 and 40." Why was forty the magical cut off? It was the expiration date on my happy milk!

I equated being forty with the end of my dating career. I've gone a few years past forty and I am happy to report that was not the case. However, prior to the big day (October 11th in case you're planning to get me something), I believed the end was nigh.

It wasn't my only worry about the oncoming milestone. Both of my younger brothers became home-owners and I was still in a tiny apartment in Los Angeles. I assumed that I'd own a home by the time I was forty, and I wasn't even close. Hell, I was having trouble paying my exorbitant rent. I had done a lot of things other people had dreamed of doing, and, in my morose mood, I wasn't counting my blessings. So, I didn't own a home; I had crossed off a bunch of other stuff off my bucket list.

I was getting closer to being forty and I didn't have my dream job yet. That was another myth. I have had some pretty cool jobs, but no matter how cool they were, they were still work. I didn't like getting up early for any of them. When the alarm clock goes off, I'll still be punching the snooze button even if I get my own sitcom.

My fortieth birthday came and went, and I survived. I even thrived. I am still single, but I'm still playing the field (I'm just glad to still be in the game). I don't own a house, but I am not paying as much for rent as I did on the dreaded day. Things are going to be fine.

Though it is several years in the future, fifty is fast approaching. I am reminded of an absolutely fabulous episode of Absolutely Fabulous; when Mo Gaffney's guest star character Bo starts to hyperventilate into a paper bag, Christopher Ryan's Marshall deadpans, "She hasn't started fifty therapy yet."

I'm right there with you, Bo. I'm right there with you.

The Fine List

They say that the truth will set you free. I'm not always so sure. It turns out that truth doesn't really belong in the workplace. In an event to not be a liar and not get fired, a person has to avoid the truth instead of out-right lie for the sake of integrity. For the sake of example I will use an old job from which I've vacated several years ago.

Sure, I like my boss. If you mean that, on most days, I would hate to see him ripped limb from limb by a wild bear, his bloody entrails splayed about like spilled spaghetti in meat sauce? Then, yes. That's the same as liking someone, right?

I was promenading down the hallway with my co-worker Barb. We exchanged pleasantries with other co-workers as we meandered to her office. Once we got there, she grabbed me and pulled me inside. Quickly, she shut the door behind me and said, "I know everyone in this building and I can tell which ones you like and which ones you don't."

I blustered that she would be wrong. I insisted, "I like everyone...equally."

I would have never gotten an Academy Award for that statement. Even as I said it, the corners of my mouth curled and I felt bile rise from my stomach.

Barb folded her arms across her chest and rattled off a list of my favorite co-workers, and then, just as easily, alternately rattled off a list of co-workers I disliked. She was one hundred percent correct and I was flabbergasted.

I looked at her like she was a witch, a real live house-haunting, broomstick riding, cauldron-stirring witch. I looked around her office for a pointy hat.

Instantly I learned her psychic abilities were somewhat self-inflated.

She explained that as we walked down the corridor to her office, co-workers would stop and say, "Hello, Mike. How are you?" To some, I replied "Fine," but to others, I replied, "I'm good. How are you?"

She nailed it. I only returned the polite conversation with the co-workers whom I liked. The others got a brisk but cheerful, "fine."

I couldn't bother to ask them how they were doing, because I didn't care. I was polite, but I didn't inquire any further into their lives. I just wanted to be on my merry way. If I instigated the "hello" it was also only followed by, "How are you?" with the nice people.

As we had walked, Barb catalogued the details, split the group into two distinctive columns and memorized the list.

In my quest to avoid being a two-faced rat-bastard, I became something worse…obvious.

Luckily, Barb was on the Good-How-Are-You List, and I could trust her. I didn't want my Fine List, which was pretty much an expletive free version of a famous list (think 'hit list' with an extra consonant), getting around.

I swore her to a secret pact.

I pleaded, "Don't tell anyone."

She replied, "I won't." Then, she placed her index finger and middle around her nose and said, "Witches' Honor!"

Snapple Stories

They say it's made from the best stuff on Earth, but I'm more interested in the bottle caps.

Bottled water is much better for you, but their bottle caps are plain white and boring. The only interesting fact you can get from a water bottle cap is the ridiculously distant future date acknowledging the water's expiration.

Snapple made unscrewing a bottle of Diet Iced Tea interesting. I've learned some peculiar bits of trivia.

Did you know that you cannot fold a piece of paper more than seven times? I tried it and, no matter what size sheet of paper, I couldn't get past six.

Only male turkeys gobble. I suppose that's an easier way of telling them apart. It sure beats lifting up their little turkey legs and checking.

According to a Snapple cap, there are 30,000 diets on public record. I will write back when I find one that works.

Disco means "I learn" in Latin. Wow. Disco something new every day.

The word facetious contains all the vowels in the English language in the correct order. And sometimes facetiously!

Mount Everest has grown a foot over the last hundred years. I sent a Sherpa up with a yardstick. He hasn't come back yet.

Antarctica is the driest, coldest, windiest and highest continent on Earth. I thought my old college dorm room was the highest place on Earth.

In 1860, Abraham Lincoln grew a beard at the suggestion of an eleven-year-old girl. Her exact words were, "Damn! You sure is ugly. Cover that shit up!"

A snail breathes through his foot. Thank goodness they don't wear sneakers.

In 2003, a six-year old girl was ticketed for not having a permit for her lemonade stand. Ironically this factoid was on the cap of a Very Cherry bottle and not on the Lemonade.

The legs of bats cannot support their body weight; that is why they hang upside down. Someone should call Darwin because that doesn't make any sense.

The moon weighs 81 billion tons. I signed the moon up for Jenny Craig, it's one of the 30,000 diets!

Africa is divided into more countries than any other continent. I have always wondered; why is Chad such a popular boy's name and Djibouti isn't?

Dim lights reduce your appetite. I must be eating with flood lights on.

International tug of war rules state that the rope must be 100 feet long. I sit on a committee for the International Duck, Duck Goose rules and regulations board, until someone yells, "Goose!" Then, I have to run around and chase them.

The world record for watermelon seed spitting is 70 feet. It's actually 68 feet and 91/2 inches. The record is held by Lee Wheelis from Texas (I looked it up). By the way, didn't you just guess it was going to be a Texan? Those Texans sure like to spit.

A ten gallon hat holds less than one gallon of liquid. I want to know, who was the guy who poured liquid into a hat? I'm going to guess it was Lee Wheelis from Texas.

"O" is the oldest letter in the alphabet, dating back to 3000 B.C. Oh! That just freaks me out that one letter of the alphabet could be older than the other. Was there a committee? "Okay. 'O' is official. We're going to adjourn for a couple of years before we decide on the rest." Of course, I'm paraphrasing because I don't know how they said anything if they hadn't decided on the letters yet.

Ketchup was once sold as a medicine. I'd like a Big Mac with Tylenol, please.

Pennsylvania is misspelled on the Liberty Bell. And it's cracked, too! I want my money back!

Drinking Snapple is my favorite trivial pursuit.

Phoning It In

When the phone rings and I get the voice mail I usually just say, "It's Mike on the phone. Just wanted to say 'hello.' Call me when you can." I realize not everyone can leave phone messages in the form of a haiku, but that's just me.

Obviously, I want to complain about people who don't know how to use the phone. Let's face it; a story about people who use proper phone etiquette won't engage readers.

When I check my messages, I get a long and pointless story from someone. I don't need all that. I just want to know who called, and maybe why. I don't want your life story. I just want to know you called. That's all. My voice mail is not a place where you can dump on me all your unprocessed thoughts and expect to get away with it. I don't listen to anyone's whole message anymore. No one has been spared my 'press seven for delete.' Not even my mom.

By the way, if I'm "in love" with you, I will listen to your whole message. I'll even save it for weeks, cluttering up my inbox. Sadly, these days, its delete, delete, delete.

Not listening to the message has backfired more than once. Let's talk about Peter. I have changed the name to protect the innocent…well…the not-always-guilty (Peter stands for Proper Etiquette on the Telephone won't Engage Readers).

Peter likes to leave long-winded messages.

"I went to the grocery store to get bananas at Shop-N-Save, but they didn't have any bananas. So, unless I buy them at another store, I guess I'm not going to be eating bananas this week. Maybe I'll check Giant Eagle. I bet they have bananas."

Blah, blah, blabbity blah.

Peter drove me bananas.

He didn't even know how to tell a story. I would have listened if he would have told a good story.

"I went to the store to get bananas, but when I walked into the store and I was the millionth customer, confetti came down, a siren blared, and now I get all my groceries, free for life! I was so happy I kissed the cashier. Her name is Edna and she's sixty-two. Yes, she is thirty-seven years older than me, but now she thinks we're engaged."

Now, that's a story. If it's interesting, I'm more likely to listen to the whole message before I delete it. A good story can be about money or sex. A great story has both, or, at the very least, a car crash.

Deleting him one time proved to be a mistake.

Several days later, I saw him in person. His first words to me were, "You missed a great concert."

I was clueless.

He huffed, "You know, the concert?"

Apparently, he left a message about a concert. I didn't know who performed. I didn't know where the person or persons played. I didn't know the price of the tickets. All of which, he outlined, was in the phone message. Somewhere in the third paragraph.

In the newspaper business we call it "burying your lead (lede)." A person starts out talking about going to Shop-N-Save and somehow ends up saying, "So instead of bananas I got apples; but on the way out of the store I noticed a poster for Ben Folds. He's going to be at the Heinz Hall on Thursday and I know a guy who can get us in."

I love Ben Folds, but I missed the show. I hadn't called him back right away, because I thought he wanted to talk about produce.

Now, when Peter calls, I listen to the whole excruciatingly long message, just in case.

HEY KIDS, LET'S MAKE UP SOME WORDS!

The English language is a curious thing. It's kinda like a soccer mom who wears Juicy Couture sweat pants. It's old but it likes to stay current. Merriam-Webster just added a bunch of hip new words to the dictionary. Just to prove it's still cool. Stacey's mom has got it going on.

Most of these new words are portmanteaus, a French word which means two words smashed together.

Here are some of the words you may encounter when you are talking to incredibly pretentious people.

Someone may tell you that they have a *vlog* or video web log. It's actually three words crammed together to make one. Trifecta! Ironically, trifecta is also a portmanteau, but it was added to the Merriam-Webster dictionary in 1974.

Vlogs are nothing more than blogs with a video component. Lots of people want you to read their *blogs*, which is only two words mashed together, but blog was added to the dictionary in 1999. It was only recently they threw the v from video in the front and made a superfluous new word.

Vloggers must be avoided at all costs. They think they're funny. They are actually just annoying. Imagine being so full of yourself you have to video record your inner most thoughts and feelings and share them with the world. I'm giving the men and women in Afghanistan and Iraq a special pass here, but I watched a vlog about a guy who was trying to decide where he was going to go on vacation. His fans got to vote on the destination. I didn't stick around to find out which city won.

By the way, you are currently reading a book and not a web log. Some of this book happens to be on the web. Any idiot can write a blog, and most do. It takes a special kind of idiot to write this book. Um. Wait.

Someone may tell you that they are going a *staycation*. This is another recently added portmanteau. It means, "I'm too poor to go on a real vacation, so I'm going to take a week off and sit around my house."

This is the most depressing of all the new words. Why not save up the days for when you can travel? Or use these vacation days to work on a special project? Paint the house! Build a garden! Write a novel! Please don't use a perfectly good week in the summer to catch up on episodes of "General Hospital" or the "Price is Right." That makes me feel sad for you.

Staycation is sadder than *waterboarding*, another new word. Frankly, I'd rather be tortured than fritter away my vacation time, sitting on the porch wishing I was in Bermuda. At least, if I was tortured in Guantánamo Bay it wouldn't be my fault. Besides, Cuba is lovely this time of year.

Some nouns have become verbs. Thanks to Facebook 'friended' is now a verb. I'll use it in a sentence: I just friended someone from high school whom I hated. This leads me to another new word, frenemy, a friend who acts like an enemy. According to Wikipedia, frenemy has been around since 1953. It goes to show you that two-faced bastards have been with us a long time.

There were around 100 new words added to the dictionary this year. Even with all those new words, Merriam Webster can still get into her skinny jeans.

Confessions of a Mathtard

My idol, Mattel's Barbie, once said, "Math is hard." I know it's not politically correct to agree with a plastic person, but I heartily concur.

Years ago, I helped my nephew Nick with his math homework. It was the worst score he ever had in math class. He actually had the right answers; but I talked him out of them. I'm not just bad in math, I'm a black hole. I suck the rightness out of people around me. The poor kid didn't even see it coming. He just respected the authority of the wrong adult.

It's not that I just can't do math; I'm a mathtard.

I couldn't find pi if it was thrown in my face by Moe, Larry or Curly.

I am really not so sure about my time's table. With a nickname like Buzz, you think I would, at the very least, memorize my seven times tables. I have never been able to play that game past fourteen, I mean, buzz.

Last year, I sent my taxes to the IRS. I was not expecting a big refund. I was both pleasantly surprised and embarrassed when I got a decent government check and a note from them telling me I did the math wrong. They made all sorts of red marks on my tax form. Apparently, I got an F from the IRS. Luckily, they didn't hand it back to me and make me do it over again.

I suppose I'll have to go to H & R Block next year. I don't want a repeat of that debacle.

It wasn't just my worst subject; I think I have some sort of numeric dyslexia.

Years ago, I was going to a party in Los Angeles. The address was on Wilshire Boulevard, a swanky section of town near Beverly Hills. I transcribed the numbers backwards and ended up in the garment district, a not-so-nice section of town. I had to call someone to get redirected. This particular time, I had the right phone number at least.

Many times I write down a phone number and get that waaa-waaa sound when I dial it. If I'm not calling you, it's quite possible you are a victim of my numerophobia. I'm going to have to get an I-Phone (it has a ridiculously cool feature where you bump two I-Phones together and the contact information is automatically deposited in the respective phones).

I don't have the problem with words, just numbers. I am convinced it's psychosomatic. I reflected on my feelings about math; and flash cards and abacuses danced in my head. It is more than just a multiplication frustration; it is a full blown fear of math. Flash cards are as nightmarish to me as rats, giant spiders, and killer clowns (thanks for that last one, Stephen King).

In high school I was in the AP English classes but in the remedial math classes.

I recognize that math is a vital language in which we communicate. You would not be reading this now if some programmer hadn't figured out how to translate these words into numbers and back into words again. I recognize the importance of math; but I don't have to love it.

When I go to a restaurant, most of my friends know to just tell me what I owe. They don't like to see the confused and panicked expression on my face when they ask me to figure out the check.

Dine out with me and tell me what I owe, you could even profit from hanging with the mathematically challenged.

Fleeing the Flea Market

After watching a commercial for "Hoarders," I decided it was time to sell off some junk gathering in the basement. That show frightens me. I am sure it motivates a lot of people to box up their old crap and send it away. I had donated a bunch of stuff to Goodwill, St. Vincent DePaul and the Veterans, but I thought I'd try to make some extra cash from my old cast-offs.

My friend Sandy and I decided we were going to go to Trader Jacks in Bridgeville; a joint venture made the idea more palatable. Besides, this way there was someone to watch over my stuff if I needed a bathroom break.

The plan was I would get there early to set up and she would join me later, since she didn't have as many big items.

Early on Sunday morning, I paid the twenty dollar vendor fee and I was directed to my spot, D 12. Trader Jacks is basically a mammoth parking lot with designated areas for people to sell their wares, mostly second hand items.

I was a little late. Seven freaking a.m. on a Sunday was considered late! As I pulled into the spot, the vultures descended on me. I got out of the car, grabbed the card table and they were at me as I was setting up.

"What do ya got?"

I opened the trunk and they peered inside. Another guy looked into the car and asked, "What's in the backseat?" I wanted to say, "A dead body. Leave me alone until I'm set up!" But it came out, "I'll be with you in one moment, sir."

I sold stuff right out of the car. Once I had a free moment, I unpacked my stuff and lovingly displayed it on the card table as I had originally planned. I took great care in positioning everything just right to maximize my sales.

That's when it started to rain. This was not going to be a good day.

I brought a bench to sit on, but almost as soon as I sat down, a guy wanted to buy the bench under my butt. What the heck, it was an everything-must-go sale. I just didn't have anywhere to sit for the next few hours.

Sandy showed up with her stuff and we were off, competing to win the attentions of potential customers. During slow moments, we tried to sell our stuff to each other. I would pluck something off my table and say, "How 'bout this? I bet you can use one of these?" She didn't buy my stuff, and I didn't buy any of hers. She did, however, sneak something into my box of junk that didn't sell.

Some really creepy looking guy bought Sandy's Lifetime movie about serial killer John Wayne Gacy (a video I bought for her for Christmas one year). I was terrified that he was going to use it as a "How to" video.

A kid came up to me and looked at the brand new still-in-the-shrink-wrap Ant Farm I was selling for fifty cents. He inquired, "Does it come with real ants?" I looked at it. "It's been sitting in the basement for a few years and I never did take the shrink wrap off...so I'm going to guess no." If it did, they would be ant carcasses by now. I thought I was going to have to put a disclaimer on it: Ants not included.

Sandy reeled in a woman who bought a bunch of her used jewelry. After the woman left, Sandy exclaimed, "She was a hoarder. I could smell it on her." I assumed that meant she smelled like dust and cat urine. Those hoarders always have a cat, usually a lot of cats. Sandy just meant she could tell the woman was a collector of unwanted items, probably cats.

Sandy had several people vying for her handbag; the one she was carrying on her shoulder. One person even tried to buy the wedding ring from her finger! I was glad her husband Bill wasn't there, because the customer only wanted to pay eight bucks for it.

We saw a lot of strange individuals on that day. Some admitted that they come to Trader Jacks every Sunday 'just to look around.' I kept thinking, "How long would it be before I saw these people on A & E's top rated show?"

If you're shopping at flea markets every weekend, you just might be a hoarder.

At eleven, the crowd dissipated, and we decided to pack up our stuff and go to breakfast.

I made $23.50. After deducting the entrance fee, I realized I made $3.50.

At breakfast, Sandy graciously offered to pay for our meal, since she made more money than I did, and I paid the entrance fee. I insisted on leaving the tip, which came out to 4 bucks. So, after spending a cold wet morning at the flea market, I was down fifty cents.

Looking on the bright side, I did get rid of a lot of stuff and I got some decent latkes (with sour cream and applesauce). Though, next time, I'm saving myself some time and dropping my junk off at Goodwill.

Barbie's Dream Kitchen

I have this kitchen fantasy; the one where I'm a good cook and I'm often entertaining friends with exotic and strange culinary dishes. In reality, if you come over, you're lucky if I rip open a new bag of pretzels.

I love going to Sur La Table. It fuels this fantasy I have where I'm a fabulous party host. My favorite Sur La Table store was in Santa Monica, blocks from the ocean in Southern California. If you're going to hunt for demitasse cups or ramekins you might as well take in an ocean breeze.

I loved to stop in and take a look around at all the nifty new gadgets.

I found eight dollar OXO corn holders. Eight dollars! My feeling is if the corn on the cob is too hot to hold, it's probably too hot to eat. I'm not spending eight bucks on something that just holds corn. It doesn't even hold any other vegetables. This particular brand didn't even look like little plastic ears of corn; I love those.

I picked up a Rustic Italian Cheese paddle. As I held it in my hand I thought, "What will I do with a Rustic Italian Cheese paddle?" I am trying to lower my cholesterol; I certainly don't need to fill this thing up with artisanal cheese from a farmhouse in Normandy. I couldn't figure out why it had to be a paddle in the first place. Was there to be some sort bizarre hazing ritual after consuming the Camembert?

I picked up a $29 whisk from Rosle. Once again, I don't beat that many eggs. Hello, Cholesterol, my old friend. Did you see the cheese and egg thingies I didn't buy? That's for you.

I have three lemon zesters. I guess I didn't need another one from Joseph Joseph. The redundant company calls their lemon peeler a Citrus Reamer. Yeah. This column has a tendency to take a turn from the mundane to the lascivious much more often than I thought it would. I personally wouldn't call my lemon zester a reamer, but then, I am not some big muckety-muck at Joseph Joseph. I don't think I could even work at a place named Joseph Joseph. The repetition bothers me.

I picked up a thirty dollar non-stick Madeleine mold pan. Thirty bucks is a lot to pay for making one particular kind of cookie. I don't like Madeleine's. They're too plain. Though, I do like the odd clam shape of them. I wonder who decided which cookies should be which shapes?

My nana used to make the most perfect cream cakes, each one looked like a three tiered dollop of Dairy Queen ice cream. She didn't use a mold.

Sidebar: When my mom and Aunt Judy made cream cakes for a recent family wedding, the cookies kind of came out obscene looking; but they were just as tasty. The cookies had a small white mound with a tan ball in the center. We called them boobie cookies. Luckily, it was an adult reception. Once again, we veer off into X-rated territory while talking about cookies. How does this happen?

There is something intrinsically beautiful about these wonderful and bizarre kitchen wares. There is something about the untapped potential of each item. There is something about imagining I could create all these magnificent things to entertain my friends and family.

I feel the same way in Staples and Office Max. If I had the right markers and the right paper, I could draw all sorts of amazing pictures to astound my friends.

It's a desire to create, to make something from these amazing tools, an unfettered desire to craft immaculate baked goods that you're not afraid to show your children.

After all, tools are the only thing that separates us from the animals. You don't see monkeys with lemon zesters and cheese paddles. Of course, monkeys so rarely entertain out-of-town guests.

How to Say Hello to a Celebrity

After years of living out in Los Angeles, I have met quite a few celebrities. Really they're just like everyone else, except they are better looking and have way more money. Oddly enough, the celebrities in this particular story are very average looking, but still talented.

I have noticed that the best way to get their attention is to wait for them to talk to you. Whatever you do, act as normally as you can and don't ask them about their movies (no one likes to talk about work even television and movie stars).

I went to an avant garde play in downtown Los Angeles. Chochata Ferrell was sitting next to me. Luckily, it was a bench and we didn't have to squish together. We are both on the big side. For the record, she's bigger than me. You will note that Ferrell breaks the 'celebrities are better looking' rule, but she does have way more money.

We talked theatre at intermission. She was very insightful (In other words, she agreed with me about the performances).

Ferrell has a dry sense of humor in real life as well (though she is not nearly as crude as her television character), and I always considered her the funniest thing on the CBS sitcom on which she is featured (they should call it, "Two and a Half Men and a Whole Lotta Woman").

A few years ago, I worked on the Independent Spirit Awards. Basically, it was my job to babysit John Waters, Dennis Hopper and a few other celebs. I had a nice chat with Nia Vardalos, the now skinny star of "My Big Fat Greek Wedding." Unlike Ferrell, Waters and Hopper, Vardalos is even more beautiful in person, but I like a nice aquiline nose.

My mom and niece were visiting a few months later and I ran into Vardalos at the Alcove, a delicious little coffee house in Los Feliz. The world's most recognizable Greek woman (Come on, Melina Kanakaredes, you know it's true) looked at me and went, "Don't I know you from somewhere?" I laughed. Usually the celebrities get asked that question, but I was having the rare reverse conversation! I told her that I worked with her on the Spirit Awards, and the memory came flooding back to her. She was delightful, and we shared some funny stories.

I got to introduce my visiting relatives to her. My mom and niece, Brittany, were thrilled that they got to meet a real life movie star on their trip. After we left, Brittany got on the phone and called everyone, "I just met that lady from 'My Big Fat Greek Wedding!'" It was late (three hour time difference) and no one cared.

On her last trip before I moved back to Pennsylvania, Brittany and I were in a record store in Hollywood. My niece was musing over a Kings of Leon CD when Jonah Hill sauntered up to her (once again, I feel I must mention that Hill is very average looking). She looked over at him and said, just a little too loudly, "Oh my God, it's Jonah Hill!" He sheepishly replied, "Hello" and she smiled back with, "Hello." The two of them had a ten second staring contest. Brittany later reported that she could hear her heartbeat thumping in her chest as she locked eyes with the "Superbad" star. Then, Brittany ran up to me and said, "Jonah Hill was talking to me." I queried, "What did you say?" She told me she ran away from him. Ring, ring. Clue phone for Brit: running away is not a good icebreaker.

I may not always know what to say when I run into a famous person, but I do know that running away is definitely not how to talk to a celebrity.

I Got a Brand New Pair of Roller Skates

My niece Chloe turned seven and we celebrated by having a roller-skating party at the venerable Pancake Skate-N-Whirl, in Pancake, Pa, a small rural town 50 minutes outside of Pittsburgh, Pa. I guess no one builds roller rinks anymore; but this one had to be really old. George Washington himself may have roller-skated there, or, at the very least, had a slushie in the concession stand.

Chloe's theme was Peace, Love and Happiness. She's quite the nascent little hippie chick at seven. It was a great theme. It was like Woodstock, only with juice boxes and cupcakes in lieu of pot and acid. The sugar hyped up the little ones more than enough. Kids, sugar and wheels is a recipe for disaster.

For the themed event, a bunch of us wore tie-dyed shirts and roller-skated. Yes, I slapped on a pair of size twelve roller skates and wheeled around the rink.

I don't want to brag; but I'm probably better on skates than I am in shoes. It's not much of an accomplishment, though, I'm pretty much a klutz on land, sea and air. I don't do badly on wheels, though. I do have to admit, I am biggest thing on wheels this side of a Smart Car.

The hardest part was trying to avoid crushing seven-year olds awkwardly darting in various directions. The kids had trouble with the Pancake Skate-N-Whirl rule, "everybody skates in the same direction." I feared for the children's lives. I was a pretty big object rolling toward them. Luckily, this is a happy story and no kids were tragically flattened in Pancake.

A couple of them hit the floor a few times. I fell once, but it was only to avoid crashing into a group of meandering children.

I nursed my wound by consuming a cupcake with a peace sign in the icing. When the kids fell, they got right back up and went at it again. I think it hurts less for them, because they're closer to the ground.

Then, the phone rang. I got a text while skating, and I answered it. I found out I could text and skate. I was surprised to learn that I could do both at the same time, too. I was so impressed by my new talent I've decided to add 'multitasking' to my resume. If there's ever an office situation where I need to roller-skate and answer texts, I've got it covered.

The one thing I couldn't do was skate backwards. My nephew Max, Chloe's nine-year old brother, is a winner on wheels. He can skate backwards, forwards, sideways. He was hot-dogging around the rink. It was really spectacular to watch. I knew he was good on ice skates, I didn't realize his talent transferred from blades to wheels.

When I attempted to skate backwards, I looked like a mime doing the "Walking against the wind" bit. It wasn't pretty.

I may have had more fun than the kids. It's been over a year since I've been on skates, and I really missed it. I used to rollerblade in Venice Beach, CA (I know, I'm a walking…um… rolling LA cliché). It was good to be on wheels again. I had a blast. It was groovy.

If you haven't gone roller-skating in a while, you ought to give it a whirl.

Terrorists Took my Fingernail Clippers

Mention "The airlines" in a comedy club and there is a collective groan from the back row. Ever since the sixties, it's hackneyed for a comedian to talk about the airlines, usually they make fun of the airplane food. Matter of fact, if any comedian tells a stale joke you're likely to hear, "That's so hack, next thing you know he's going to do ten minutes on airline food."

It is with some trepidation that I bring up the subject of the airlines.

We are never going back to the days before 9/11. It's been ten years and it is still sinking in.

I now know I'll never be able to take food from home on an airplane. I can't bring a bottle of water from home, but I can buy one at the Au Bon Pain in the airport for about as much as I paid for the whole case at Costco or Target.

If I want to go somewhere overnight, I have to buy Good News disposable razor blades when I land, unless I want to check my carry-on.

They are minor inconveniences of the new world order. I just keep forgetting. I'm curious about the amount of shaving cream, disposable razor blades and fingernail clippers the Travel Safety Agents have collected. Is it going to a giant land fill? Are the sales for fingernail clippers and Swiss Army Knives on the rise?

I hope no one is using recycled fingernail clippers. That's just gross.

My neighbor was telling me he buys a new pocket knife every time he comes back from vacation, because he keeps forgetting to take it off his key ring. To the TSA's, a bottle opener is a weapon.

It's a sorry-ass terrorist that will have to say, "I'm going to shake this beer bottle vigorously and then you're going to get it. Oh wait. It's not a twist off."

I kind of resent having to take off my shoes. I never remember to wear something that slips on and off easily. I'm thinking bunny slippers for my next flight.

I understand that, with my swarthy Mediterranean looks, I'm always going to be profiled. I try not to giggle every time they rub that metal detecting wand over my body, but I'm severely ticklish.

I was strip-searched in Greece because I hadn't shaved. I guess they thought I was a native trying to flee to America. To be fair, it was the night after a bombing at an American hotel there. I had to stand in my underwear in a room while security guards went through my stuff. I could see them judging my souvenirs. It was the kind of situation you only see in porn movies, except it never got naughty, just humiliating.

Here's the thing, not long ago, I watched an eighty-year old woman get the terrorist treatment near the United Gate. The only bomb she is going to drop is going to be in her Depends.

I guess they can't discriminate. Instead they treat everyone like terrorists.

We're in a "assumed guilty until proven innocent" world now, instead of the other way around.

I just wish I could remember all of it before I go to the airport.

Artists and Their Models

While flipping through the pages of a Woman's Day magazine, in the bathroom, at my mom's house, I noticed something.

Those people at Women's Day are sort of douchey. They showed this fabulous dessert on the cover; a raspberry cheesecake with swirls of shaved white chocolate on top and a cascade of bright red raspberry's rolling around on a stark white plate. Inside the magazine, it's all diet tips, exercises and low calorie recipes!

What a tease!

It's the classic bait-and-switch. Oh, yum, cheesecake...wait a minute...it's really yogurt and Cool Whip!

Apparently, a lot of women's magazines do this. They lure you in with a sweet treat on the cover, but then show you 101 simple tricks to keep the pounds off. Yeah. Right. Diet tip number one: Don't look at the covers of women's magazines! They'll make you salivate.

My favorite, another issue of Woman's Day, has a picture of bright multicolored cupcakes on it with a giant banner that reads "Splurge," followed by an article entitled, "Easy Ways to a Healthy Heart." Hello, Mixed Messages!

I went to the local newsstand and started skimming women's magazines. I really wanted to tell the newsstand vendor, "Leave me alone, I am doing research," because I was getting funny looks. I guess he didn't know I wasn't going to wear any of the clothes I found in Women's Wear Daily. So, I decided to look at just the covers. Newsstand vendors don't like it when you look inside and don't buy anything, but they're even more suspicious of men reading women's magazines.

The covers show dessert on a lot of them, except O Magazine, which has the picture a smiling African-American woman on it.

She was on the heavy side. I wouldn't think a picture of a large African-American woman would sell many magazines, but she looked sort of familiar.

With the exception of O, most of the others, that didn't have dessert on the cover, had women in one-piece bathing suits. Also, the yellow tape measure was a popular prop.

Sidebar: Prevention Magazine isn't a woman's magazine but it is clearly marketed for women. It's also smaller and more light-weight than most magazines. It is pocket-guide shaped. No one knows why. I guess an ounce of Prevention is worth a pound of Cure(also a magazine title).

Food always looks so pretty in the magazines. Even food I personally think is disgusting makes a nice picture. Maybe because I've been away from meat for a long time, but McDonalds makes their food look spectacular. Though, nothing they sell in the actual restaurant (and I use the word restaurant loosely) looks anything like the commercials. That bright red tomato and crunchy-looking Romaine lettuce sticking out of the bun look particularly appetizing. It doesn't look at all like the wilted iceberg and shriveled tomato slice I've seen on their actual burgers. Though I've been a vegetarian for quite a while, I've been to McDonalds and seen the food firsthand (I traveled from Los Angeles to Pittsburgh by car; Mickey D's had the cleanest restrooms).

Domino's has the "Show us your pizza" campaign. The idea is that the consumer takes a pizza picture, mails it in, and the best picture wins money. Apparently, even Domino's can't make their pizza look good in ads. Basically, they've given up.

The photographer must have thrown up his hands (probably after throwing up some of the pizza), and screamed, "I can't do it! I can't make it look like food, let alone pretty food!"

Most of the time in food modeling the food pictured isn't actually food I'd want to eat. Most of the sweets are made from fondant which is a sugar, corn starch, gelatin and Crisco, which just sounds gross. Back in the day, ice cream was cold mashed potatoes and food coloring. It sure makes a pretty picture, though. Pretty enough to eat.

The Further Adventures of a Name Dropper

Over the years in Los Angeles, I've came to know a bevy of big names and hung out with some recognizable D-Listers (my dinner with Sinbad, for instance), but it was always fun to spot a celebrity.

Warning: Watch out for falling names, I will be dropping a lot of them.

I was once on stage at the Comedy Store performing when Emilio Estevez, Charlie Sheen and a cluster of beautiful women entered. In retrospect, I imagine the famous brothers rented the women (this took place before Denise Richards came in and out of Sheen's life). I was thrilled that big time movie stars saw me on stage.

It was one of my earliest celebrity encounters, and I will not forget it. They watched my act, saw a couple of more comedians and took off. I didn't get a chance to talk to them. Like every stand-up comic, I really only had one question for them, "Did you like my set?" Vanity thy name is comedian.

After one performance, a guy walked up to me and shook my hand. He said he liked my act. I talked to him for a while and realized he looked vaguely familiar. His name was Joe E. Tata, also born in Pittsburgh, PA. Joe is most known for his recurring role on the original "Beverly Hills, 90210" where he played the Nat, the owner of the Peach Pit. Not an enormous star, but my first brush with celebrity.

I was sitting in my favorite breakfast eatery when a friend who turned to me and said, "That's Orlando Bloom over there." I looked around and asked, "Behind the lesbian?" He responded with, "No. He is the lesbian." Bloom has very soft features and he was wearing a checkered flannel shirt and bandana on his head; a clothing choice I've only seen on bespectacled sporty women in smart vests and sensible shoes.

Once, I almost took out Matt LeBlanc and his car door. I was driving up La Cienega Boulevard and he hopped out of his car suddenly. I almost hit Dianne Keaton on Wilshire Boulevard and Larry King walked out in front of my car in Beverly Hills. Actually, I starting to wonder how I never accidentally killed a celebrity.

My most surreal moment came in the car wash in West Hollywood. The car wash had a long hallway filled with pictures of celebrities who had used the car wash. I was looking at a picture of George Hamilton and joked to my friend Ralph, "Do you think he really comes to get his car washed here?" At that moment, George Hamilton walked in. I turned to George and pointed at his picture and said, "I guess you really do get your car washed here!"

Mr. Hamilton smiled politely. His teeth looking particularly white against his perma-tan.

Since then, I've hung out with David Spade, Tim Meadows, Adam Sandler and a host of big names and small ones, regulars from SNL, Reno 911, and comedy clubs, and we've had small, quiet conversations. The kind you would have with anyone at a party. The only difference is. . . I didn't have any trouble remembering their names the next day.

Even though I played it cool, deep inside me there's still a little Lucy Ricardo trying to get out. Luckily, I never set fire to my fake nose in front of William Holden or stolen John Wayne's handprints from the front of Mann's Chinese Theatre.

COMEDY, ALCOHOLISM AND SOMETIMES Y

After performing stand up in comedy clubs for several years, I have learned all the various descriptions of comedic styles, there's the prop comic, the wise-ass, the klutz, the intellectual, the blue collar comedian, and a variety of others. However, there are really only two kinds of comedians; alcoholics and recovering alcoholics. Trust me, if you find yourself in Los Angeles, you will meet more comedians at an AA meeting than you will at the Improv.

Much like the letter Y, I was an exception to the rule, but then I was never as famous as Blank, Blank or Blank (the second A prevents me from mentioning their names).

One of LA's hottest AA meetings was held at the Log Cabin in West Hollywood, conveniently located near the Abbey, one of LA's hottest bars. It doesn't take Alanis Morrissette to digest that delicious bit of irony. Let's just say if you were going to fall off the wagon, you could do it while sipping an Appletini at one of the swankiest joints in town.

I was never an alcoholic, but I did have a history with hooch. By the time I started standup comedy, I had already been through my drinking phase.

Actually I did all of my best/worst drinking when I was under age. After I turned twenty-one, the thrill of poisoning myself into a happy stupor was gone. I didn't stop just because I was legal; when I was nineteen I drank an entire bottle of vodka and a half a jug of orange juice. I was sick for a week.

My friends read off a laundry list of things I had said and done, none of which I remembered. All of them were far too embarrassing to mention. I will reveal that I ran my fruit-of-the-looms up a flagpole and recited the pledge of allegiance to my underpants (surprisingly, there were far more embarrassing items on the list). It was only funny because I didn't die.

It put me off drinking for a long time. Actually, it put me off orange juice for a long time, too. Whenever someone mentioned the word 'screwdriver' I ran screaming from the room. I couldn't even watch home repair shows.

It must be a common side effect of the extreme hangover experience: One of my best friends got drunk on peppermint schnapps and it was years before she could even look at a candy cane, and I know several people who think Goldschlager is the German word for "projectile vomiting."

I've met a lot of comedians who start stories with "This one time I was so drunk…" A humorous anecdote would follow. However, most of the stories ended with vomiting, a scary one night stand, or, "I woke up naked in my neighbor's front yard, hugging the lawn jockey."

It's hard to work in a bar, especially one with a two drink minimum. Comedy Club owners have never imposed a drink maximum, and that's why their rolling in it.

The Bagel Experiment

In our family, like many families, we take over food to a house when a loved one dies. My cousin Bob's mother-in-law passed recently. My mom made pasta and chocolate cookies. Since I wasn't planning on cooking anything, I brought over a dozen bagels.

Two days after the funeral, I found two bagels (one pumpernickel, one plain) under the passenger seat of my car. The two bagels must have fallen out of the bag when I made a sharp left hand turn.

I posted a comment on Facebook, "If Bob was wondering why he was shorted two bagels from a baker's dozen (13), it's because I found two under the passenger seat today."

My cousin Cindy promptly wrote back, "He probably didn't even notice."

I got to thinking, like I do, Bob would have noticed. Not many people would, though.

If I gave a dozen to my brother Rick, he would have counted the bagels. He would have interrogated his children on which kid ate which bagel, "Who took the sesame?" It's not that he's curious. He just likes to agitate his children.

If I handed a dozen bagels to my brother Brian on Saturday, Sunday morning he would see them in the kitchen and exclaim, "Hey. When did we get bagels?" Let me make this clear, he's not a stoner; he's just oblivious to unimportant things like the days of the week. Go ahead, ask him what day it is. I'm sure he'll look skyward and start counting backwards from Sunday (because that's when he went to church).

Bob would have known how many bagels were in the bag. So, I wondered how his brothers and sisters would react if I gave them a bag of eleven bagels.

His sister Elaine wouldn't have known. She would just go, "Bagels! Yummy!"

His brother Ray wouldn't have known. He would probably hand them back and say, "Thanks, but we're not doing carbs this week."

Bob's sister Patricia would know, too. She would know exactly how many and which kinds of bagels were in the bag. Bob and Patricia are just detail-oriented.

I wouldn't be surprised if Patricia froze them individually, so she could take one out each day. I imagine she would even write on each freezer bag, "blueberry," "cinnamon-raisin," "garlic," and "plain." I wouldn't even be surprised if they were in alphabetical order in her freezer! Okay. She's VERY detail-oriented.

Even with four young children of his own, I would imagine Bob took the time to count the bagels. Or several days later, he would (in his head) list which child ate which bagel and realize they were short two, knowing it was a baker's dozen of thirteen and not twelve. I am sure he was wondering, "Why would Mike buy eleven bagels? Did he take two out for himself?" That's why I had to let him know.

It became an interesting sociological experiment. Who would know? Who would care? Why? It became an interesting game of how each person would react. Whether they would react as I imagined, or if they would react completely the opposite of how I imagined.

This experiment works great with bagels, since they come in a bag. You get thirteen donuts but you can peer into the box and notice how many are in there. Obviously, it wouldn't work with a dozen eggs or a six-pack because you could see the empty slot for the missing one. Though, I love the idea of giving someone five beers, eleven eggs, or a Whitman's Sampler with one chocolate missing (preferably the caramel).

By the way, most people would throw out a bagel if they found one or two under the passenger seat several days after they bought them. With that in mind, here's my latest sociological experiment: Who would eat the car bagel?

Can't Talk Now, I Have my Foot in my Mouth

Everyone has embarrassing moments. I seem to have more than my fair share. If there was an award for saying the wrong thing at the wrong time, I would have the crown, tiara and sash.

I can surely stick my foot in my mouth. I've turned it into an art form.

Last year, I was covering the theatre beat for a couple of Los Angeles papers and websites, writing reviews. I was going to two or three shows a week. Therefore, I was bumping into actors all of the time. I bumped into my friend Drew at a show and we started discussing local shows. He asked me what was hot in theatre.

I had just seen a production of *Hamlet*. The performance was staged at the Hollywood Forever Cemetery on Santa Monica Boulevard. It was sort of creepy and cool seeing a play at night in a cemetery. They actually had an open grave for Act 5, Scene One, the gravesite scene where Hamlet finds the skull of the old court jester, Yorick.

Drew inquired, "What did you think of the play?"

I said I had pretty much liked it. Drew then said, "I had a friend in the play."

This is where my mouth got out away from my brain. I blurted out, "I hope your friend wasn't Polonius, Polonius was awful. I don't know why they cast this guy!"

I did an impression of this dreadful actor, reciting dialogue from the play. I bent over, wagged my finger and spouted out, "Neither a borrower nor a lender be..."

He didn't stop me right away.

His friend was indeed played Polonius. Of course. It could only have been Polonius. I disliked one actor in a cast of forty, and it was Drew's best friend.

A month later, I ran into Drew during an intermission at a Groundlings show on Melrose Ave. And somehow I've managed to put my foot back into my mouth. Everyone was milling about sipping wine or soda when I saw him in the crowd. He was standing with a friend when I wandered over to him.

I joked, "Remember when I told you that your friend in *Hamlet* was awful. I did a Polonius impression and everything."

I turned to the friend, "You should have seen it. I skewered this guy."

Guess who the friend was? Polonius. Naturally. I didn't recognize him out of his costume and make up. There is some sort of Murphy's Law in effect when you have this dread speaking-without-thinking disease. The person is always nearby. I got to put my foot in my mouth twice, on the very same subject.

When you're an actor, you are expected to be able to receive criticism, but not on a night out with friends. By the way, he did read the review I wrote and he had some choice words for me, too. Actually, he balled up his fists and proceeded to tell me what he thought of me.

Intermission was ending. Drew just sort of pointed at the blinking lights and tinkling bell, and said, "Well, we better get back to our seats." He grabbed his friend's arm and hurried back into the theatre. Someone call Mario Lopez, because I was literally saved by the bell.

It's Not Special if It's the Same Special

Christmas is fast approaching and soon it will be over. We will wake up on December 26th and get back to our regularly scheduled lives. You will still find a stray pine needle in the house, or find a small piece of wrapping paper, a sparkle, or a tangled red ribbon and it will be sad. The best thing about Boxing Day is that I will not have to watch anything on television, at the multiplex, theatre, or concert hall about Christmas until next Thanksgiving.

I don't want to sound like Ebenezer himself, but I hate "It's A Wonderful Life," "A Christmas Carol" and "The Nutcracker." Don't even get me started on "Rudolph the Red-Nosed Reindeer!"

I didn't always hate holiday movies, shows and specials, it's just I've seen them year after year. If I hear the tinkling sound of Tchaikovsky, my nerves are set on edge.

My cousin Nicole was in the Nutcracker. I loved seeing her the first year she danced out from under the skirt of the Sugar Plum Fairy. We went again the next year, and the year after that. I'm just saying, can't we have a different ballet at Christmas? Can someone throw a Christmas tree in the background of Swan Lake and call it a holiday show?

Besides, that Herr Drosselmeyer gave Clara a nutcracker for Christmas? I hope that girl doesn't have a peanut allergy like most kids I know.

As far as "It's a Wonderful Life" goes, I am just so sick of it. I love Jimmy Stewart; but I despise George Bailey and hope that the next time he offs himself, he stays dead. Jump, George, Jump! Worst of all, I hate that mean old Mr. Potter, who steals the money and gets away with it! What the heck is that? They never catch him. Instead, the townspeople rally around the Bailey's and bail them out with their own hard-earned cash. It's supposed to be sweet and sentimental but the bad guy gets away. Where is the justice?

Rudolph drives me crazy. In the Rankin/Bass stop motion television special Santa is so mean to Rudy before he uses him as a flashlight. Dear Santa, get some headlights on that sleigh(The little St. Nick according to the Beach Boys), and stop abusing mutant reindeer. Also, why was Heat Miser so cranky? In 2006, I had a lovely 101 degree Christmas in Palm Springs. What's wrong with a little heat at the holidays?

The worst offender is Charles Dickens. I can see that when Charlie wrote "A Christmas Carol" back in the day they were pretty short on holiday tales. But come on! That movie is on television every year, and there's like ninety-five versions of it. Ira David Wood, Reginald Owen, Richard Kiley, Tim Curry, Patrick Stewart, Albert Finney, Bill Murray, Scrooge McDuck, Jim Carrey, The Muppets, Barbie, even, have all been Scrooged.

Every sitcom character in America had a close encounter of the Christmas kind. Mr. Magoo, Bugs Bunny, Fred Flinstone, George Jetson, Alex P. Keaton, Al Bundy and Dr. Who were all visited by ghosts past, present and future. Cyndi Lauper and I are sick of the same old story.

Yes, Virginia there is a Santa Claus, but you knew that last year and the year before, so buck up.

When I was ten, I remember being very angry at Susan Walker from 34th Street. Santa finds her dream house! I got Rock 'em, Sock 'em Robots that year and I believed in him the whole time!

I know I sound like I should live high above Whoville with a little dog, but I love Christmas. I just don't like repeats and Christmas television is ninety percent reruns (Speaking of Rerun, I'm sure he was visited by three ghosts on "What's Happening." Hey. Hey. Hey. I would bet a giant pair of red suspenders on it).

I will be grateful for January. Though it will be bitter cold and there won't be as many days off with pay, I'll be glad to slip back into the routine and discover something new in film, theatre, and television.

In other words, have a Merry Christmas and all the other crap that goes with it.

Code Talkers

I got a text the other day and I had to call in a Native American Wind Talker to decipher it. The acronyms are getting out of hand. I think it's time we joined the AAAAA, the American Association Against Acronym Abuse.

It all started with Laughing Out Loud. LOL is the most common of the text messages I receive. Maybe because I'm funny.

A few years ago, when the whole bizarre thing started, I asked a friend, "What's Rotful? Did something go bad in your refrigerator?"

My mind played Vanna White and added a vowel. I assumed it was some derivation of awful. That it was "rot-filled." It made sense in my head. I thought I was being insulted; it turned out the person on the other end of the keypad was laughing. ROTFL was Rolling on the Floor Laughing.

Then I got ROTFLMAO and my response was WTF?!

It was bad enough during the eighties when the personalized license plate craze took off. I remember following cars around just hoping to figure out what their license plate meant.

C LOVR. This guy in the Pontiac Catalina either likes four leaf clovers or the ocean?

Once I pulled up to a Volkswagen Beetle and asked, "What is T2UL8R?" And the response was, "Talk to you later." Since the light turned green, I didn't even realize that my question was answered. I thought I would have to get the answer from him at a later date.

Now I find myself staring at my phone hoping to decipher the code.

I was Instant Messaging my friend Jason who wrote BRB, and I couldn't figure it out. It took him several moments before he answered me. It meant Be Right Back. If I knew that I would have waited much more patiently. Instead I wrote, "What does this mean? Are you still there? What's happening?"

CYA is both "Cover Your Ass" and "See Ya." I guess it depends on the context.

BTHOOM is not an onomatopoeia. It means Beats The Heck Out Of Me. I'll use it in a sentence: Question: What does this text mean? Answer: BTHOOM!

DAMHIKT or Don't Ask Me How I Know That.

Really?! Does DAMHIKT come up in a sentence so often it needs to have its own acronym?

"So-and-so has a mole on his/her ass. DAMHIKT."

I think merely by saying "Don't ask me how I know that," we already know the answer.

I also got "Meet me at *$." Asterisk Money? Star money? Star cash? Oh! Star bucks!

I even found a bizarre abbreviated code on a menu. I was trying to figure out what EVOO meant. It wasn't the band that sang "Whip it" in the 80s. It turns out EVOO is the new shorter way to say Extra Virgin Olive Oil (Blame Rachel Ray).

And one day, after corresponding with a friend for several minutes I got, "CIAO." It took forever to decipher. See eye Ay Oh? Is your Seeing Eye Dog laughing his ass off? I couldn't quite grasp it. But then I realized that sometimes a goodbye is just a goodbye.

Ciao.

Bad Santa

On Christmas morning, I was on the phone with my Aunt Terri in Virginia. She lives in a nice little apartment not far from the beach. I was wishing her a happy holiday when she said, "Do you hear what I hear?" It was Christmas after all, but she wasn't singing a carol. It turned out she had her own Little Drummer Boy next door. She remarked, "It sounds like Pearl Jam over here."

Apparently, Santa Claus brought her neighbor a full drum set under his tree. She said the boy had been banging on them all day, but my aunt, a Youth Services Coordinator in a library, would never complain about a child doing anything. She is their biggest advocate.

You have to wonder why a kid in an apartment would get a full set of drums for Christmas. Someone wasn't really thinking.

I sympathized because when I was living in my tiny apartment in Los Angeles, my upstairs neighbor got a full weight set one Christmas. It sounded like I lived beneath a bowling alley the entire month of January. Luckily, he ignored his New Year's resolution and stopped working out by February.

I couldn't be too mad, though. I have been accused of being a bad Santa, too. One year, I gave my cousin Nicole a talking stuffed animal. It repeated back whatever you said to it. It was cute for the first ten minutes.

Months later, I remember my Uncle Jim saying, "Oh, thanks for that lovely Christmas present, by the way." He was being one hundred percent sarcastic. The doll kept squawking.

A year later, after he hid it in the garage and forgot about it, he had frightening encounter with the thing. He was getting ready to leave the house one afternoon when his wife, my Aunt Judy, called out to him, "Where are you?"

He yelled back, "I'm in the garage."

Then, he heard a distorted voice repeat, "I'm in the garage."

The batteries were dying and it had a slow distorted sound, "I'mmmmm innnnn the gggggaaarrrrraaaageeee."

He had completely forgotten about the doll. He feared it was a masked killer mocking him. It scared the hell out of him.

The call is coming from inside the house.

Of course, when I heard the story, I laughed and laughed. Then, my neighbor got the weight set. Proving the old adage, "What goes around comes around."

I was in the programming department at the Disney Channel not too long ago. We were in a skyscraper on West Alameda in Burbank, but we moved our offices down from the twelfth floor to the sixth floor. My friend Gail had that same talking stuffed animal. She packed it up in a box of her things.

When we returned to the new offices the next day, the stuffed animal lay next to the box with the batteries removed. Apparently every time the movers lifted the box, it talked back to them. It scared them, too.

Here's hoping that next Christmas there are plenty of Silent Nights!

Past, Present and Future

I am writing this to you from the past. Though, it's currently my present. Actually, since I will more than likely rewrite this essay several times before you see it; this means it's in both my past and my present. You guys are in my future.

I wish I could send myself tonight's lottery numbers.

Some people claim they can look into the future. I've met a few psychics in my time and almost all of them were living just slightly above the poverty line. You would think they would have fat stock portfolios and be too busy breaking the bank in Vegas to worry about my love life.

However, on a few rare occasions, I was convinced I was talking to someone who saw the future, or, at the very least, a glimpse of it.

Once, over twenty years ago, I went to a Psychic Picnic in the North Hills of Pittsburgh. This was long ago when I was living at home with my mom, dad and two brothers, Rick and Brian. It was before GPS and I got a little lost. The psychics managed to find the right grove, but they were probably using their special abilities.

I went to meet with someone who specialized in psychometry. This person's gift involved touching of physical objects to get a 'reading,' Usually the item was gold, silver or some metallic object like keys. Nothing cheap. I kept thinking, maybe this is how she makes her living, by stealing watches, jewelry and cars.

I hastily grabbed my watch from the nightstand and went off to meet with her. The woman's name eludes me. Sadly, I do remember that it wasn't a "Bewitched" name like Esmeralda, Tabitha, or Endora. It was much more mundane, like Jane, Sue or Betty, which is kind of disappointing when you think about it. I wanted an exotic name with my psychic.

Anyway, I gave her my watch and she held it. She started getting a visual image and described it to me. "You will meet a red headed woman in a white car. You probably already met her. She is very important to you. You will marry her."

I hadn't met a redhead. I wasn't interested in anyone at the time and pretty darn sure I wasn't about to get married anytime soon. I thought her cauldron was short a few toadstools.

Later that night, I relayed the story to my mom. My mom said, "Your brother Rick just went out with a red head and she drove a white car. Funny."

That's when it occurred to me to ask my brother an important question, "Rick, did you borrow my watch last night?"

He snapped, "You weren't using it! How did you know?"

He always did that thing where I felt bad for accusing him of taking my stuff, even though he took my stuff.

I shrugged and said, "It's totally okay. I just wanted to know." I said "totally" a lot back then.

He shrugged, "Yeah. I took it. What's it to ya?" Yes. It was now my fault that I angered him for questioning him. Let's skip over the fact that he borrowed it without asking.

The odd thing is; he wore it when he went on a date with a red head in a white car.

That redhead is now my sister-in-law. Rick and his wife, Vickie have been married for over twenty years now (I really don't want to know the exact number, I feel old enough as it is).

So, the psychic picked up on my brother's energy somehow. There was no way she was just reading my body language, because I didn't even know Rick went on a date with a red head. I don't know what a skeptic would say to convince himself that this woman was somehow a charlatan (I'm pretty sure I'll find out in the near future…cause maybe you're the skeptic reading this right now).

I just know it happened, and I have a beautiful niece and handsome nephew that remind me that there was some kind of Rick and Vickie energy on that 'borrowed' watch.

The only thing I really know for sure is that if you live with relatives… lock up your stuff!

TV Guidance

I picked up the TV Guide one day and I was reading it at breakfast. The blurb for the season premiere of Wipeout states, "Contestants tackle obstacles, including the Snowplow Sweeper and the Big Balls." I laughed so hard, oatmeal came out of my nose.

Someone said to me, "Television is getting stupider."

I responded with, "Television has always been stupid."

Exhibit A: "My Mother the Car." Jerry Van Dyke, Dick's little brother, buys an antique car that speaks to him through the dashboard with the voice of his deceased mother, Anne Southern. It's one of those wacky supernatural sitcoms from the sixties.

Exhibit B: "Cop Rock." A musical police drama. Picture the kids in the Glee club going to the Police Academy! Hilarity ensues! When a group of Hispanics are summoned for a line up, they sing, "We're the local color with the coppertone skin / And you treat us like we're guilty of some terrible sin."

The real sin here was committed by the writers and the producers. Personally, I love to sing about the serial rapists, murderers and creeps.

Who gave the green light to "The Cavemen," a show about the Geico cavemen from the television commercials?

How about "Holmes and Yo-Yo," a comedy about a robot police officer?

Does anyone remember "Small Wonder?" Another robot show. This time the titular wonder is a robotic little girl. The robot grew in the third season and they had to pass it off as a systems upgrade. Really? This was a television show? And it lasted three seasons?

By the way, if you are a television exec and you hear the word 'robot' in the pitch, walk away, man. Walk away.

In the defense of television, I watched every episode of "Gilligan's Island." We knew it was stupid; but we watched it anyway. Phil Silvers (Harold Hecuba), Hans Conried (Wrongway Felman), and Kurt Russell (Jungle Boy)all visited the island, met the stranded Minnow passengers, and left them there. They had a lot of guest stars for a show about people stranded on a remote island.

I used to watch "The Partridge Family." I always used to think Shirley Partridge was a slut. Look at those kids. Not one of them looks like one of the others. I mean she had a dark haired son, a brunette daughter, a red head, and don't even get me started on those little ones!

Newton N. Minow once called television a 'vast wasteland,' and that was all the way back in 1961.

I love sitting in front of the boob tube, but it's not called that because of "Baywatch" reruns.

Every now and again, a show will come along to inspire, create, and teach in a marvelous new way.

Think about all the people who have lost weight on "The Biggest Loser." Love the show or hate the show, it has changed lives. Yes, the trainers plug Subway sandwiches and chewing gum, but they have also altered the lives of many of their contestants.

Last year, I watched an episode "The Biggest Loser" while eating a Snickers bar. Apparently, the message wasn't getting through. This year, however, I am exercising to the show.

Every reality show has the sniping and bitching, but I really watch it to see the bodies transform. It's very inspiring.

Minow, in the very same speech, also said, "When television is good, nothing — not the theater, not the magazines or newspapers — nothing is better."

Pass me the remote. I'm going treasure hunting. Yes, I'll find a lot of dirt and bile before I get there, but I still want to watch.

Oh, good Lord. "Jersey Shore" is on.

Nutty Health Foods

I thought it was high time to get healthy. There's only one problem with it. I resent being treated like I'm health store illiterate.

A few weeks ago, I spoke with a Nutritionist. First of all, she was overweight. Second of all, I told her I was a Pescatarian and she stared at me like I had two heads. I had to explain that I was a vegetarian who ate an occasional piece of fish. I assumed a Nutritionist would know this; but I guess the old aphorism is true, "never assume, because you make an ass out of u and me."

I got my comeuppance, though. I went into a health food store and the counter girl started talking about goji berries, acai, carob, flax seed, wheatgrass, etc. My head was spinning. Did they just discover this stuff in the Rain Forest or what?

I learned that Gluten-free is good, but free radicals are bad. So you can free the whales but not the radicals. I'm not sure why. I think they run around in your body committing acts of terrorism. They cause aging. If I were free of free radicals, would I look like I was twelve? I'm not sure. I'm not sure I'd want to reverse aging so much that I couldn't ride Space Mountain.

I am not completely dysfunctional in the health food store. I have taken shots of wheatgrass; it sort of tastes like ice-berg lettuce juice.

I had heard about flax seed before, but I never trusted words that end in x. They all sound so science-fictiony. Flax. The more you say it the less it sounds like a real word. I don't even like looking at it.

Chia seeds are new to me. When I inquired for more detail I learned that chia seeds were actually chia seeds! You know those little seeds you plant on your clay Garfield? Yes. Apparently, they are rich in Omega-3's. You can eat them right off your chia pet.

Maybe I'll get the one that looks like Scooby Doo. Next time you're in the health food store ask for more information on Ch-ch-ch-chia seeds.

When you go to the Health Food store, take notice. You must be up on the latest nuts, seeds and berries or you are deemed antioxidant illiterate. What am I? A well-read squirrel? Am I a chipmunk storing acorns for the winter?

Sometimes I don't feel healthy enough to go into the health food store. They are full of arrogant disdainful Employee/Philosophers. I recently encountered one. Even her t-shirt was smug… it insisted, "Go Green!" It didn't want me to just recycle; it ordered me to recycle. "Go Green!" I blame the exclamation point mostly. They spout about sprouts and they look down at us mere Pescatarians. The smug woman at the counter said to me, "You haven't gone completely vegan yet?"

I guess if you're going vegetarian, you have to go whole hog. So to speak.

The ego of the health food store employee astonishes me. I want to tell her that yes, she will live longer than me, but she will do it while working her whole life in a health food store.

Man cannot live on yogurt raisins alone. Every now and then you have to get a scoop of ice cream or reach for a handful of French fries. I'm just saying

Misty Water-Colored Memories

My memory isn't what it used to be. Today, I went to push my glasses up on the bridge of my nose, but I had already taken them off earlier and I poked myself in the eye.

I walk into rooms and I forget what I'm doing there. Usually, I stand there for several seconds, walk back out, remember and return.

My life is a scavenger hunt. I am constantly hunting down, my keys, my wallet, my tennis shoes. For me, "Why am I here," isn't an existential question; it's a literal one. Why am I here? Oh. Right. I left something important in here.

Gone are the days when I could run out of the house at the last minute. I have to mark off my checklist, denoting the location of my money, keys, cell phone. Once, I was talking on the cell phone as I was walking out the door. I grabbed my pants pocket. I almost said to the person to whom I was speaking, "Wait. Where is my cell phone?" I have also sought out my glasses while they were on my head, and I have looked for my keys while I was driving.

I am convinced my tennis shoes have gotten up on their own power and walked out of the room where I left them. Maybe they were bored, because I don't exercise enough in them.

The forgetfulness is really bad in this era of personal identification numbers and passwords, especially because so many of them have to be different lengths or contain numbers or symbols or both. I will never meet the love of my life on Match.com simply because I don't remember my password. There is probably someone out there yearning to meet me, but that person is on the other side of a wall. I can't communicate with my suitors; I can only wink at them. Pyramus and Thisbe be damned.

I like the websites that give you hints. I responded to the one that read, "Name your favorite high school teacher and your favorite author." I used William Weprich and Walt Whitman, because the alliteration made it one step easier for me. I was still denied. I had to put my teacher in as Mr. Weprich or it wouldn't grant me access. I think I changed my favorite author to Constantin Cavafy. Yes, I picked another poet, but I actually like alliteration more than poetry. Even though no one was going to see it but me, I couldn't tell the truth and name my favorite author as Stan Lee, the creator of Spider-Man, the Fantastic Four and the X-Men. I had to be pretentious even when no one was looking.

Sometimes the hint questions are different and I am tripped up even further. "Name your childhood pet." I had a turtle. He didn't have a name. He was just Turtle. Maybe he was even Turtle the turtle. He only lasted a few days and then he ran away. Or rather walked away. After all, he was a turtle. Though now, years later, I suspect that when my dad said, "The turtle ran away" what he meant was, "I flushed him down the toilet."

I was trying to make a point about something, but I forgot what I was talking about.

Facing up to Facebook

Things are about to get metatextual. I saw the Oscar nominated movie, "The Social Network," the other day and I wanted to write about it. Yes. This is a column about a movie about a website. When I share this column on Facebook, the serpent will swallow its own tail.

If you haven't seen the movie, it paints an almost villainous portrayal of Facebook creator Mark Zuckerberg. Zuckerberg is portrayed as a Harvard hacker who made it big because he wanted to punish his ex-girlfriend for dumping him. Somehow he goes from sociopathic to social networker. It's a well crafted film, but it is a little hard to reconcile the seemingly benign social networking site with the conniving hoodie-wearing Zuckerberg. Still, I'm not logging off Facebook anytime soon.

I have to admit I'm a bit of a Facebook fanatic. I like to Post. I like to Share. I like to Like. There should be a Facebook twelve-step program.

For the record, I don't shoot people in Mafia Wars, I don't save little lost lambs on Farmville, and I don't stake vamps in Vampire Wars. I just I like to check in and see what my friends are doing. I don't Foursquare either, though. I don't really see a reason for telling people I'm watching a play at the Off the Wall Theatre (right in downtown Washington), shopping in the Strip, or hanging in Shadyside. I see no reason to make life easy for my stalker. He has to go through my garbage and guess my whereabouts like the stalkers of yore.

I do want to point out a petty annoyance I have about the social networking site. Hey. It's me. I'm full of petty annoyances.

Here's the thing; I'm not exclusive. I will accept all friends on Facebook. I don't care. I'm a club that anyone can get in, but if you befriend me (by the way, "befriend" is an actual verb, "friend" is not), and I don't know you personally, please have a face picture as your profile picture. Is it that too much to ask? It's called Facebook, after all. It is not Shirtless-TorsoBook. It is not Cute-Picture-of-Your-Cat-or-Dogbook. It is not Favorite-Cartoon-Characterbook. It's Facebook. Face!

I like to see a face. I don't care if you are knock-a-buzzard-off-a-dung-wagon ugly. Just have a face picture as your profile picture.

By all means, take pictures of your washboard abs, your adorable cat and/or dog, and do post jpegs of your favorite cartoon character, but show me your face. If I can post a picture of my big bulbous head, than you can, too!

You can use those other pictures for your profile over at MySpace. It's just bands, DJ's and comedians vying for your attention on MySpace; they don't care what you look like as long as you buy their CD, come to their club, or buy a two-drink-minimum at their latest gig.

Speaking of MySpace, I'm a little sad for my first friend over there, a Mr. Tom Anderson. He must miss us all terribly.

We all left MySpace at the altar and ran off with Facebook. I, personally, did have a brief, casual encounter with Friendster and got acquainted with LinkedIn, but I would never feel the same way about them as I do about Facebook.

Next time you're on Facebook, remember Randy Newman's immortal words, "You have a friend in me." If you're desperate, I'm on MySpace, too, begging strangers to come to my next comedy gig.

Another Monk Moment

I saw her cough into her hand from across the Verizon showroom floor. Two minutes later, the Verizon manager handed me my new cell phone. She extended her hand, waiting for me to take it and shake it. I was paralyzed with fear. It is what my friend Sandy calls, "one of my Monk Moments."

Sandy was not referring to the cloistered men on mountaintops who twist pretzels and jar jellies. No. She was referring to the titular detective of late night cable, Adrian Monk. A character so germophobic he makes Howie Mandel look like Charlie Brown's friend Pig-Pen.

I did take the Verizon manager's hand and gave it a firm shake. Then, I said to her, "I noticed you have a bottle of Purell back there behind your computer. Might I have a squirt?"

She handed me the bottle and I quickly defended myself against her germy fingers. Seriously, didn't she see that thing about coughing into your sleeve? It's all the rage, these days.

I have to admit I do have several Monk Moments a week. It is not fear; it is self preservation. This winter I had a flu that wouldn't go away. It lasted about eight days and it came with all the requisite side effects, runny nose, coughing, headache, stomachache, and one too crass to mention in a family friendly book.

In order to flee the flu, I've been 'extra-careful' since it ended. Read: A big giant 'fraidy cat.

I read an article that people who ride the bus are twice as likely to get sick as opposed to those who drive into work. Though I was convinced that the article was written by the top executives in BP, Shell and Exxon, I still fear my fellow bus patrons.

The other day, a woman on the 38c sounded like she was going to hack up half of her lung. Though I was several rows away, I wanted crawl out the window. This was on the way to downtown! I had to spend the whole day worrying about catching her illness.

If you sniffle, I will leave you. I've parted company with dear friends because they started to sound like they were coming down with something, and I didn't want to go down with them.

I saw a sign reminding people, "If you're sick, stay home." Do they listen to these wise words plastered on billboards and bus stops? Hell to the no.

Please, if you're feeling under the weather, stay there. Under your dry roof. Get under the covers. Catch up on your favorite soap opera. You probably haven't tuned in since high school. Of course, I'm convinced daytime television is meant to drive people back into work. If I'm going to watch people lie and back stab each other all day, I might as well do it in my cubicle where I can get paid for it.

If you stay home, I won't look like such a coward when I am walking around in my wellness.

A Walk in the (Ross) Park

In another effort to economize, I found a cheap alternative to the health club/gym treadmill. I have taken to long walks in the woods. Like many writers before me, a long walk in the woods is inspiring. However, due to the inclement weather in Western Pennsylvania, I have taken the path less traveled. I've left the yellow wood and started mall-walking.

On sunny days, you'll still find me out on the open road. I've walked several beautiful trails in Pennsylvania and California (the trails in Griffith Park are still my favorite). I have even walked the scenic High Line trail in New York City, a floral oasis in an urban jungle. However, throughout the winter, I'm hanging with the seniors at the mall.

It is exercise, but it is far from a walk in the park. Though, you will find 'park' in the title, i.e., Ross Park, Parkway Center, there is very little flora and fauna. Even the name, "South Hills Village," conjures up the image of a small bucolic town. Clearly, they are misleading monikers.

Let's set aside Parkway Center Mall for a moment. Nestled high on a hill above Pittsburgh, it is a nearly defunct shopping mall. Walking around there is like starring in your own post-apocalyptic zombie movie, only the walking dead are my fellow mall walkers.

I accumulated vast store of knowledge on my journey, doing laps around Robinson, Ross Park, Parkway Center, South Hills Village and the Galleria, all in an effort to spice it up by trying various locales. However, every single one of them looks the same on the inside. I could probably be plopped down in a mall in any state in America and find the Abercrombie and Fitch store while blindfolded. Hint: It's one of the few stores in which you have to step up to get inside.

The mall walkers are easy to recognize. They are near ancient men with grim determination and a jaunty gait and no packages or bags. Occasionally you will see an older man with a bag and a slow pace. Don't be confused, he's an actual shopper; the hapless victim of his wife or girlfriend, waiting for her to come out of the lingerie store.

It's a strange juxtaposition at the mall: The geezers hiking about and the young 'tween girls. Instinct kicks in early for the prepubescent girls. Their gathering skills must be deeply embedded in their DNA. They come out of Justice, A & F and Hollister loaded for bear.

I think I have learned more about fashion than I did about exercise.

After ten laps, five upstairs and five downstairs, I decided to vary my view and actually wander into some of the stores. In A&F they will greet you as if you were in a Benihana in the mid-to-late eighties. All cheerfully yelling "Hello!" at you as you walk by each employee. Also, plaid is back. Why? If I wanted to look like a lumberjack, I'd carry an axe.

Here's a handy tip for future mall-walkers: Don't go in the Coach store. Those women will descend on you like vultures and relentlessly peck at you until you purchase something. I escaped with a tiny key fob, the cheapest item in the store.

I can't imagine what would have happened to poetry if Ralph Waldo Emerson and Henry David Thoreau came out of the woods and into the malls for their daily constitutionals (not that I would ever compare myself to them). Thoreau would have gone from White Pond and Goose Pond to the White House/Black Market. Maybe Emerson would have given up on Self-Reliance and written about the Cinnabon.

Though, I suspect Emerson who could find God everywhere, would have even found him at Hollister, looking cute in a puka shell necklace and faux-Hawaiian shirt.

The Public Broadcasting Blues

Almost as soon as you mention The Public Broadcasting System, people assume you're pretentious. I am not one of those I-only-watch-PBS-People, but I do like a few things over there on channel 13. I have very eclectic tastes and no DVR. It was really hard for me to pick between "Masterpiece Theatre" and "Family Guy," but when PBS advertised the magnificent Maggie Smith on their show, I opted for "Masterpiece." Plus, if you pick "Family Guy" you get stuck with "The Cleveland Show" or worse, the rarely-as-funny "American Dad!"

The Public Broadcasting Company is having some trouble these days, and I thought I would urge people to support their local PBS station, except they do a few things that bug the heck out of me.

Don't get me wrong, I'm hard on PBS, because I care. If I were blindly watching a rash of reality shows, I wouldn't care at all what WQED was doing. There's no reason to be tough on TBS or Spike, because I'm not watching anything on their channel.

Here's the thing: When you say, "This program was paid for by a generous grant from the Exxon Corporation" is it that much different than a commercial? I am sure it's not going to be an Alaskan travelogue about oil-stained polar bears.

By the way, has the United Kingdom not made any new sitcoms since "Are You Being Served?," "As Time Goes By," and "Keeping Up Appearances?" I realize they are popular and funny shows, but enough is enough. Dame Judi Dench must be getting hella royalties. They play the same six episodes of "As Time Goes By" in an endless cycle on PBS; and it's about as funny as a Marmaduke cartoon. I know, because I have tortured myself by watching each episode over and over again. What can I say?

I'm a masochist. I'm even sick of Mr. Humphrey's and Missus Slocombe from "Are You Being Served?" It's time to retire a show when there are no living cast members (Mollie Sugden and John Inman are going to haunt me, I just know it).

I would love to see some other BBC programs (programmes) other than these beloved 70's britcoms.

Hey PBS, how about throwing us a French or German television shows? At the very least, I would love to see something from this century. You got me spoiled when I saw the modern retelling of Sherlock Holmes. First of all, the actor's name is Benedict Cumberbatch and I just like saying that. "Have you seen the new Sherlock Holmes played by Benedict Cumberbatch?" It sounds slightly naughty. Say it with me, out loud, "Benedict Cumberbatch."

However, they are still broadcasting ancient episodes of "The Lawrence Welk Show" over there. I detested the big band man thirty years ago. He has not 'grown on me,' which is odd when you think about how much I like to blow bubbles. My teeth clench whenever I hear, "And a' one and a' two."

I fell in love with "Downton Abbey," a vedy British show about a wealthy family and their multitude of servants, mostly because of the wickedly funny aforementioned Maggie Smith. I fell in love with the show when the immutable Ms. Smith said, "What, pray tell, is a weekend?" One of the best lines ever spoken by an upper-crust dowager.

I guess I'll end up pledging after all. Besides, "Masterpiece Theatre" keeps me from watching guys getting smacked in the groin by their two-year-old on "America's Funniest Home Videos."

The Truth About the Tooth

I lost my front tooth at Seven Springs, a ski resort in a picturesque part of Pennsylvania. I also sprained my rib tumbling down the mountain in a snow-tubing accident. The incidents, however, are unrelated.

Snow-tubing is for thrill seekers who are too lazy to go skiing or snow-boarding. Basically, you ride down a hill in an inflatable tire with handles. Most of the time, you go flying down the mountain alone. Sometimes, you join together with a group of friends, interlock your tubes, and sail down the hill. It's a blast.

Two friends and I joined our tubes together and we went down one of the bumpy slides. After a big bump, I was airborne and let go of the handles of my friend's tubes. As I disengaged from my friends tubes, I flipped over several times, thus injuring the rib. Had someone been filming it; I am pretty sure it would have been a marvelous YouTube clip. Alas, the event was undocumented. I get a sharp pain in my side whenever I cough, sneeze or move to fast. As I am a larger person, I don't move that fast that often.

I have been telling people that the tooth loss and the rib happened in the same time. This isn't true. It's true that I lost the tooth at the aforementioned ski resort. It's also true that it was during the snow-tubing event. The way I tell it, I sound like a daring adventurer. That's not really how it happened.

Here's the truth about the tooth: I lost it while on the conveyor belt on one of our many jaunts up the mountain. I broke my front tooth while tearing into a packet of hand warmers. Even though I had gloves on, my fingers were cold. I didn't want to remove the gloves to take off the cellophane wrapping, so I used my teeth. Big mistake. My tooth and a small piece of cellophane wrapping went flying off into the snow.

My friend, also named Michael, said, "We should look for it." He's one of the most intelligent guys I know; I don't know why he thought we could find a white tooth on a white capped mountain on a moving conveyor belt. I'm chalking that up to concerned-for-a-friend rather than a-synaptic-misfire-of-neurons.

My other friend on the trip, Ryan, found the whole thing to be hilarious. He claimed I looked like the Wicked Witch in "Snow White and the Seven Dwarves." Had I a poison apple, I would have given it to him. With his I-phone in hand, he tried several times to capture a picture of me with my mouth open. Most people who know me should assume this would be rather easy, but I was talking with my hand over my mouth like I was trying to keep a secret from a lip-reader.

By the way, the Wicked Witch in her apple vendor drag was not the only Disney comparison that was made. Until the tooth was repaired, I whistle when I talked. As my cousin-in-law, Danny, pointed out later, "You sound like Gopher from Winnie the Pooh." And I do. I need a miner's hat and I'll be all set.

While I sound like the beloved buck-tooth rodent, I'm half-a-buck short. I look like a fat hockey player.

My main problem is that I can't say words that start or end with the letter "F." Believe me, I found out my new verbal disability rather rapidly, as words that start with the letter "F" flowed freely (ffflowed ffffreely).

I'm offffff to the dentist. Next time you see me, I hope to be my bright smiley selfffff.

WHAT HAPPENED TO BUBBLE GUM?

I ran into Walgreens the other day. I had to buy the usual Walgreens-type stuff, batteries, a copy of the Observer-Reporter (No, I have a subscription...I was getting an extra copy, yeah... that's it...an extra copy), and bubble gum.

The gum was crucial. I was trying to stave off the death breath I had from my garlicky breakfast bagel. The "Everything Bagel" is the perfect morning food for indecisive Librans. I don't have to pick between poppy seed, garlic, salt or onion...I get Everything! Who said you can't have it all?!

I just had a few moments to choose a chewing gum. I was already late for my next appointment. You never know I might be thrown into a situation where I had kiss someone (it could happen!).

I scanned the display of black packages of gum. My choices were Rain, Cobalt, Swerve, Prism, Vortex, Solstice, Flare and Elixir. Um. What? Was I in a foreign land? Nope. I was on Banksville road. It doesn't get more American than Dormont/Beechview, unless you count all the Italians who live there.

What happened to bubble gum? Where were my old friends, Spearmint, Peppermint and Juicy Fruit?

When did gum go high concept?!

I asked the girl at the counter, "What is this?"

She picked up a package of Swerve and said, "Swerve." Apparently she thought I was illiterate. I retorted with, "Yes. I can see that part. What is it?" She said, "Chewing gum."

Clearly she was not up to the task of deciphering the package. I needed a Chewing Gum Rosetta Stone. Though, I'm not sure what my face would look like if someone did explain it to me. I'm guessing I would have made that same contorted expression my redneck friend did when I explained sushi to him. His reaction was, "Sushi ain't food, its bait. It's what food eats before it becomes food."

I had the same sort of what-sort-of-high-falutin'-bull-puckey-is-this-face as I stared down at the little black package of gum. I was on the side of the bumpkin's in this one. It was the sort of advertising campaign stunt that makes the fly-overs hate New York and Los Angeles. Let's call peppermint Cobalt. Let's call spearmint Rain. Whatty what now? I can't imagine being in the boardroom with those Madmen as they laid out a PowerPoint presentation on the renaming of gum. Let's make chewing gum hip and cool. Let's put it in a unique black package with neon colors on it. Let's make chewing gum look like it's going out for an evening of martinis and nightclubbing.

Cobalt, Rain, Solstice…etc. They all sound like dance clubs in Vegas. I would dance at a place called Cobalt. I don't necessarily want it in my mouth.

While I stood there in the store I noticed that on the side of the package, in small print, Swerve said it was, "a tangy sweet tropical flavor."

Okay. I'll bite or, rather, chew. I bought the gum and, to my eternal regret, I liked it. Now I'm going to be one of those jackasses who buys Swerve, Vortex, Solstice and Rain instead of Doublemint, Juicy Fruit, and Bazooka Joe.

For the record, the whole point was moot. No one did kiss me that night, but I kept my Swerve on, just in case.

WHITE LIES

They say that "Honesty is the best policy," but I think that it's a lie. Sometimes telling the truth can get you into deep water.

Any guy who has ever heard the sentence, "Do I look fat in this dress?" Knows whereof I write.

By the way, there is no good answer to that question. Never say, "Not just in THAT dress," or, even, the seemingly innocuous, "You look beautiful to me." It implies that you like fat women. Or, possibly, fat guys in dresses depending on who originated the question.

You may mean, "You look beautiful," but the woman (or whomever) hears, "You are huge, but I love you this way." If you ever plan on answering this question, get ready for the shouting and crying. I have found the best policy is to feign deafness or pretend you are really, really concentrating hard on something, like a television commercial; "Sorry. I was watching this. They have 0% APR fixed financing at that furniture store you like." Anything to change the subject. I have known guys who have ran from the room when this sentence rears its giant, puffy head.

You may have heard the phrase, "Nothing but the truth, the whole truth"...blah, blah, freaking blah. I have run across a lot of people who have told the truth but probably should NOT have disclosed the whole truth.

Once, a friend of mine who happens to be a high school principal told me this story: A teacher called up and said, "I can't come to work today I have a venereal disease."

Um. I am thinking the word 'sick' would have worked fine there. Worse. The teacher elaborated, "I have to lie in bed with my feet in the air."

I only thought, "Isn't that how you got this way in the first place?!?"

A long time ago, I temped at the Post Office on Pittsburgh's Northside. I worked with a guy named Whitey. I believe he was an albino. He had Ghost white hair and Bible paper skin. As I said, it was a long time ago and 'political correctness' wasn't really 'a thing' back then.

I would hesitate to call him friend. I would even find it difficult to call him a co-worker. He really didn't like to work, and he didn't really like anyone at work. He was also very ornery. I think because people called him Whitey. So, for that, he can be forgiven.

Anyway, I was standing next to the supervisor when Whitey walked up to us and said, "I have to go home. I [pooped] my pants." He used a much more crass euphemism for defecation.

Once again, this is a time when I think you could be less truthful. I think an "I'm sick" would have sufficed. Anything would have been better; "I'm sick," "My kid is sick," or "I left the coffee pot on at home and I have to run back and switch it off."

When Whitey made his startling announcement, a sickening pallor overtook the supervisor's face (not unlike Whitey's natural shade). I am not sure what my face was doing at the time, but I know I was shocked.

I would like to tell you that we were concerned for him and that we didn't laugh at him or mock him in anyway. But that would also be a lie.

Wedding Crasher

A few weeks ago, I crashed a wedding. I was in Virginia Beach/Norfolk area and I was going to a benefit concert at the Chrysler Museum. Semi-legend and Disco Diva Pamela Stanley ("I'm coming out of hiding," "If looks could kill," among a few others) was performing. I had met Ms. Stanley a few times (in Rehoboth Beach, Delaware) and I thought it would be fun to go to her show since I happened to be in the Tidewater area at the time.

At seven, there was to be a cocktail reception before the concert at eight. I wore a decent pair of jeans and a nice shirt for the occasion.

I parked at the Museum and even though I saw a group of people going in the back door…I went in to the front of the building. The front door was locked, but there were people milling about on the patio, smoking. I went up to them and noticed the men were wearing suits and the women were in elegant cocktail dresses. I pulled on the patio door and it was locked. Two people from inside were coming outside to smoke and they held the door for me and a friend of mine to enter.

I saw waiters running around with hors d'eouvres. I assumed it was the cocktail reception. I thought, "Gee, we are getting a lot of bang for a twenty-five dollar ticket."

Some guys were wearing black bow ties. I started to feel embarrassed by my clothing choice. We were the only ones in jeans. I turned to my friend, "I guess since it's a benefit people get dressed up?" I was thinking it was awfully formal for a fifty-something B-List Disco performer.

I looked at the tickets and thought, "Maybe I have the wrong night, the wrong venue…something!? It didn't say 'black tie' on the ticket."

When a waiter asked me if I wanted something to drink I thought, "Well, this must be the right place."

We started to get funny looks. I was getting more and more uncomfortable. My friend wasn't even as dressed up as I was. He was wearing faded jeans and a pullover sweatshirt.

On my way to the men's room, I noticed a gift table. I thought, "I read that they were having a Chinese auction. Do they usually wrap the gifts in such fancy paper?"

I was inspecting the gifts. In retrospect, I'm glad the bride didn't happen by at this moment to wonder why I was fondling her presents."

It was taking me a while to clue in.

I turned to my friend and said, "I think we're at a wedding." Sadly, my friend was even more obtuse than I. I really ought to start traveling with people who are smarter and better dressed.

Some woman was looking at me and smiling. Then she turned to her friend and started talking. The two of them shared a laugh. I got a little angry because I was convinced that she was talking about me. I realized it wasn't paranoia when I saw her point at me, that sly way, under her cocktail napkin as she lifted the drink to her mouth.

Finally, a woman with a walkie-talkie was cruising through the museum. I asked, "Excuse me. Is this the Pamela Stanley concert?"

She smiled graciously and told me we were, indeed, in the wrong part of the building. She escorted us through the building to a separate wing. We passed the wedding party on the way to the other wing. They were getting their pictures taken by the Greek and Roman statues at the museum. I smiled to the bride and she smiled back. She was probably thinking, "Did I invite that guy? Why didn't he dress up for the occasion?"

I hope I didn't end up in the wedding album. I'll forever be a question mark over the happy couple's head whenever they take a stroll down memory lane, "Who was the guy in jeans?!"

The woman from the museum unlocked a door, opened it and gestured, Carol Merrill-style. We entered the concert hall, and I was finally among denim-wearing Pamela Stanley fans. I pushed out a heavy sigh of relief.

My advice; "Always dress up when you're going out. You never know when you'll accidentally end up at a wedding."

Casting a Spell Check

Technology is a wonderful thing. I love my computer and I'm glad I don't have to type this out in a typewriter with three crinkly carbon copies behind it. Though, I realize I have been relying on my technology a bit too much. Take spell check, for example. It's not an excuse to avoid learning how to spell.

Actually, spell check and auto correct can be dangerous things. I am having several problems with it. It's bad enough that for years every computer I touched kept trying to change my name from Buzzelli to buzzard. It happened in an e-mail once and a friend of mine started calling me Buzzard. The nickname stuck for a few people. I don't mind Buzz or Buzzy but I don't like Buzzard. Maybe if the actual bird were a little bit more photogenic.

Once, I was working as an administrative assistant at The Walt Disney Company. Basically, I was a secretary, except I never got flowers on Secretary's Day. My boss asked me to reschedule a meeting. I sent an e-mail. I had misspelled inconvenience. Unfortunately, I hit 'send' and the auto-correct spell check feature changed it to incontinence. Yes. The last line of my e-mail said, "Sorry for the incontinence." I was waiting to hear back from the Senior Vice President of Marketing. I was terrified I would get a response that said, "I don't know what you've heard, but my bladder is fine. Thanks for asking."

Luckily, I was able retract the e-mail before the executives saw it. One advanced Outlook program nearly ended my career there and another saved it. Ah, technology!

I've also had a few problems with the auto-correct function on my cell phone. Several embarrassing things have popped up, odd, disturbing word choices. Words I don't normally use in everyday conversation, unless I'm talking to truck drivers.

A simple auto-correct mishap caused consternation when I was texting a friend; the word 'as' became 'ass.' Apparently my friend thought I was going to see a play called, "Ass you like it." William Shakespeare writes a porno.

I'm not the only one suffering from the auto-correct craziness. There is a website devoted to auto-correct malfunctions called, appropriately enough, "Damn you, auto-correct!" Most of the offensive incidents are too naughty to mention here.

Some of the more innocuous ones involved celebrities. Puff Daddy's real name is not Sean Combover. Kelly Pickler, of course, became Kelly pickles.

One of my favorites involved a woman who wanted to write, "I was sitting on the dock enjoying my day." The auto-correct changed dock to a vulgar word referring to a male appendage. The response texted back from their friend was, "That does sound like an enjoyable day!"

Another changed the word vinegar to a female body part and someone was very confused by an ingredient in their salad. Let's put it this way, Eve Ensler never wrote monologues about vinegar.

I overheard a woman say, "Stupid cell! I sent pictures of my puppy on the phone...the auto-correct changed the word puppy. Obviously, my mom did not open the attachment."

Resume became rectum. Imagine a human resources recruiter making that mistake in an e-mail; "I need to have your rectum on my desk right away." I wonder if they got the job.

Heed my warming...um... warning. Avert catastrophe and learn how to spell.

Below Average Genius

I'm not smart enough to hang with the intellectuals, but stupid people annoy me mightily.

I'd be a genius on "Wheel of Fortune," but a dummy on "Jeopardy."

Seriously, does anyone watch both shows? I get so frustrated when I watch the "Wheel" and Vanna has overturned almost all of the tiles and the contestants stare blankly at the game board.

One particular episode made me sad for America. The gameboard read, "_ood-burn_ng stove" and the contestant yelled out, "Food-Burning stove!" Yes. I happen to have a food burning stove, but it's not a real thing, or, at least, not a something that would be a "Wheel of Fortune" answer.

The next contestant shouted, "Hood-burning stove." It took the third contestant to ask for a 'w' before he could work out the answer. By the way, if you haven't guessed by now, the answer is "wood-burning stove." Maybe none of these contestants have ever had a vacation rental in the Adirondacks. None of them were likely to win one on the show, either.

There are hundreds of YouTube clips of really stupid people talking to Pat Sajak. I don't know how he can stand there and smile at them. I'd be like, "Seriously!?! You didn't know that? We practically spelled out the entire thing. God, you people!" Clearly, I'll never get a chance to host "Wheel." The closest I've gotten to the "Wheel of Fortune" is a nickel slot machine in Las Vegas.

The disparity of knowledge within the thirty minutes between "Wheel of Fortune" and "Jeopardy" is literally mind-boggling.

A half an hour earlier, over on Jeopardy, someone had to come up with the answer to this gem: "He was the last grand master of the Knights Templar." The response was, "Who is

Jacques de Molay." That is the question, isn't it? Who the heck is Jacques de Molay? How many Knights Templar can you name? If I were a contestant, I would probably blurt out, "What the hell, Trebek?" At least my answer would be in the form of a question.

That Alex Trebek is so smug, too. He only knows the answer because they are printed on tiny index cards on his podium.

How about this Final Jeopardy question: "This cheese was created in 1892 by Emil Frey and named for a singing society whose members loved the cheese." None of the contestants answered correctly, "What is Liederkranz." I have to concede that it's pretty tough question. I don't think I've ever spread a Liederkranz on a cracker. I can only name a few cheeses anyway and as far as I know cheddar, havarti, Swiss and goat were never singing groups. By the way, Frey is also credited with creating Velveeta. Apparently, he was a real cheese whiz.

So, sadly I can't play Jeopardy. I'm just "Wheel of Fortune" smart. I'm trying to turn that into a pithy phrase. I'll use it in a sentence, "Oh, don't be too hard on him. He's only 'Wheel of Fortune' smart."

I do know the answer to some excellent Trivial Pursuit questions. "My Little Margie" was played by Gail Storm, and the largest waterfall is Angel Falls in Venezuela. However, I haven't memorized my new bank account number, and I don't know where I put my car keys.

I don't want to be an intellectual, but I don't want to be an idiot either, and God forbid, I don't want to be considered just normal.

I guess I'm a below average genius.

www.ingramcontent.com/pod-product-compliance
Lightning Source LLC
Chambersburg PA
CBHW071511040426
42444CB00008B/1589